handmade
STYLE

23 MUST-HAVE
BASICS TO STITCH,
USE, AND WEAR

ANNA GRAHAM

Published in 2015 by Lucky Spool Media, LLC
www.luckyspool.com
info@luckyspool.com

Text © Anna Graham
Editor Susanne Woods
Designer Rae Ann Spitzenberger
Illustrations Amy Hibbs except where noted
Photographs © Anna Graham, except:
Photographs pages: 1, 4 (left), 6, 8 (bottom
row and top right),12-25, 28-29, 36-37, 38-39,
46-47 © Holly DeGroot

The information in this book is accurate and
complete to the best of our knowledge. All
recommendations are made without guarantee
on the part of the author or Lucky Spool Media,
LLC. The author and publisher disclaim any
liability in connection with this information.

9 8 7 6 5 4 3 2 1

First Edition
Printed in USA

Library of Congress Cataloging-in-Publication
Data available upon request

ISBN 978-1-940655-06-2

LSID 0023

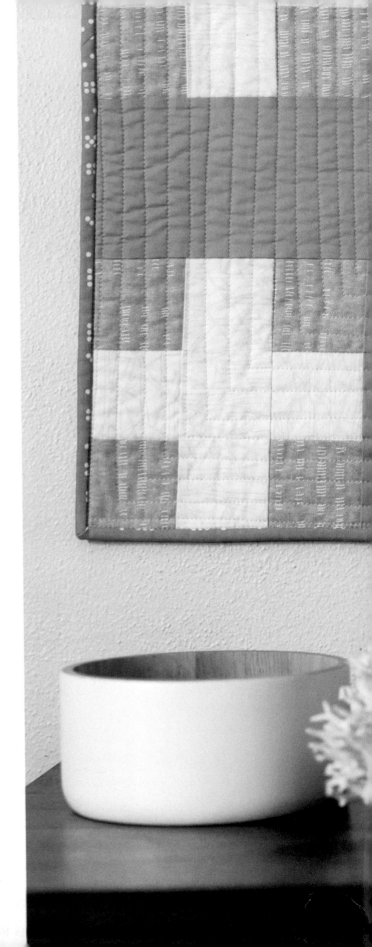

This book is dedicated to my
daughters, Natalie and Emily, I
want you to know that you can
do anything if you put your mind
(and heart) to it.

contents

introduction

I WANT YOU TO BE ABLE TO MAKE THESE PROJECTS AND HAVE THEM
reflect *your* style. I think that's one of my favorite things about sewing —
being able to make something you love just how you want it. I've always
been drawn to making things myself because I could customize to my
heart's desire: colors, patterns, and quality. I hope you'll find this
collection one that piques your interest. My goal is that you will sew a
dress, make a tote, or finish a quilt and be as excited about the finished
product as you were about making it. And while you're at it, why not
share the love and make gifts for everyone you hold dear? Deep down,
when I'm making something for someone else, I feel an amazing sense
of enjoyment that I just can't seem to find anywhere else. I'm so glad
you stopped by! Grab a cup of coffee, sit down with a friend, and get out
your must-sew list.

In this book if you come across terms within the text that are new to
you, take a look in the Glossary at the back.

I always suggest tracing pattern pieces instead of cutting out the
originals, all of the projects with pattern pieces indicate to trace the
pattern pieces first. You never know when you might need to make a
change. Or worse, lose or damage the original.

I think you'll find within these chapters many projects you'll love
and use — and make them your style.

chambray dress
page 65

flip–flops
page 68

women's tunic

page 71

metal bracelets
page 74

to carry

zip top tote
page 76

pencil case
page 82

tablet case
page 80

market bag
page 83

gadget case
page 86

bucket bag
page 88

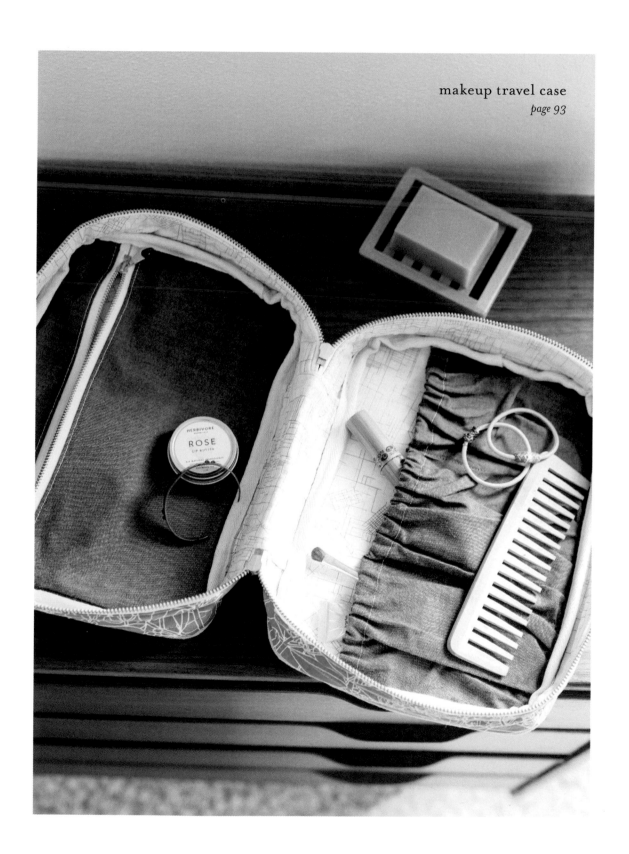

makeup travel case
page 93

gingham tote
page 102

rainbow clutch
page 108

to use

picnic plaid quilt

page 112

up & down quilt

page 114

arrow quilt

page 116

roll-up picnic blanket
page 118

floor pouf
page 120

pillow set
page 123

carry-all pincushion
page 130

`<>` quilt

page 133

patchwork bench
page 136

MAKING AND ATTACHING DOUBLE FOLD BIAS TAPE

Bias tape, you either love it or hate it. Most store-bought bias tape is made with polyester, which is durable but not the softest option. I like to make my own. I love how you can pick exactly the fabric you want to coordinate with your project.

A bias tape maker comes in so handy for speeding up the process. I use a Clover 25mm (1") bias tape maker most often. It makes 1" single fold binding or ½" double fold. You can also make straight grain binding.

To make ½" wide double fold bias tape, you'll start out by cutting 2" strips of fabric (the manufacturer suggests using 1⅞" strips, but I find either work well for me) on the bias (meaning a 45-degree angle to the selvage edge). By cutting on the bias, the fabric takes on a new life: it'll be able to bend and curve around corners with ease! You could also make straight grain binding using 2" strips of fabric cut across the grain, from selvage to selvage. If the project you're working on doesn't have curves, you can save fabric by cutting straight grain binding.

Join the 2" strips by placing the short end of each strip at a 90-degree angle to each other, right sides together. Mark a diagonal line from one corner to the opposite corner. Sew on that line. Trim the seam allowance to ¼". Press seam open or to the side and repeat to join as many strips as you need.

To make double fold binding, feed the continuous strip through the bias tape maker. Use the dull side of a seam ripper to start feeding the fabric in. Use a hot iron and spray starch and your bias tape will be nice and crisp! To finish, take the single fold bias tape you just made and press it in half again, but this time press the one folded edge about ⅛" from the other folded edge.

To apply bias tape, first unfold the tape. Press the short end to the wrong side by ½". Using the side of the bias tape that was folded shorter, align raw edge of bias tape to raw edge of project. It's best to start attaching the bias tape in an inconspicuous spot. I like to start it at a side seam or a less noticeable area of a project. That way, the extra little seam won't stand out as much.

Starting at the fold, sew along the first crease. You'll work your way around the entire project. Take your time. To ease the bias tape around a tight curve, gently stretch the tape to fit the curve. It sometimes can help to press the bias tape to mimic the curve before you begin sewing. You may also find it helpful to clip into the outside edge of the bias tape by about ¼" every ½" or so to help ease it around a curve.

Once you reach where you began, overlap the bias tape and backstitch. Flip the tape around the raw edge and over the stitching line you just created. Topstitch using a longer stitch length (3.0mm) along the inner fold.

the projects

CHAMBRAY DRESS

This casual and easy to wear dress will be the one you pull from your closet over and over again. The comfortable envelope-style neck makes it not only easy to get in and out of, but makes setting the sleeve quick and painless. Three-quarter-length sleeves with cuffs and bias tape trim complement the neckline, and the patch pockets make it perfect and practical to wear for any occasion.

style tips

▸ This will be a summertime staple, but pair it with leggings and leather boots and you have a classic fall look.

▸ Make the bias tape from a small-scale floral print or even a solid so that those details really pop!

MATERIALS
Lightweight fabrics such as voile, seersucker, chambray, lawn, or rayon:

58" wide fabric: XS-S 2⅛ yards, M-2XL 2¼ yards

45" wide fabric: XS-M 2¾ yards, L-XL 2⅞, 2XL 3 yards

3 yards of ½" double fold bias tape OR an additional ½ yard if you are making your own (see page 62 for making bias tape)

3 yards of tracing paper (Pellon 830)

CUTTING
See pullout for pattern pieces. Cutting diagram (see page 142) and Size chart (see page 140). Trace and cut the pieces for your desired size.

(1) Dress front

(1) Dress back

(4) Cuffs

(2) Sleeves

(2) Pockets

SEAM ALLOWANCE
½" unless otherwise noted

FINISHED SIZE
XS–2XL

instructions

Transfer all markings from pattern pieces.

SEW DART
1. On dress front, align dart legs right sides together. (A)

2. Sew from raw edge to dart point. Do not backstitch at dart point; instead, tie threads together. (B)

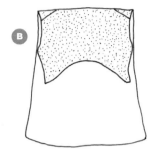

3. Repeat for other dart.

4. Press darts toward the bottom of the dress.

PREPARE NECKLINE
1. Staystitch neckline on both front and back dress pieces. (C)

2. Working from wrong side of fabric on the back piece, unfold the bias tape and align raw edge to raw edge of dress neckline. Sew along first crease. (D)

3. Press bias tape up and away from dress. Refold bias tape over raw edge of neckline. Press in place just covering previous stitching. Sew along inner fold of bias tape.

4. Repeat for front neckline.

MAKE POCKETS

1. Press top edge WST by ½" then again 1½". Edge stitch along bottom fold. Press side and bottom raw edges WST by ½". (E)

a.

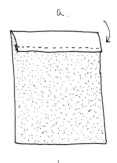

b.

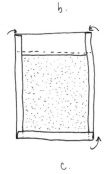

c.

2. Pin pocket in place as indicated on pattern piece. Topstitch along both sides and bottom of pocket. Reinforce pocket by sewing a small triangle at the top of each pocket, continuing down one side, across the bottom of the pocket, up the remaining side, and finishing with another triangle. (F)

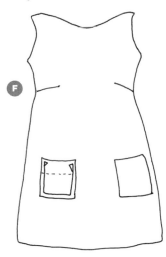

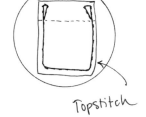

Topstitch

SEW SIDE SEAMS AND SLEEVES

1. Place front and back pieces RST. Align side seams matching notches. Sew from the bottom of the underarm to the bottom of the dress along both side seams (G). Finish seam allowances as desired (see Tip, opposite page).

2. Align sleeve underarm seam RST, matching notches. Sew. Finish seam allowances as desired (H). Press seam to one side. Turn sleeve right side out.

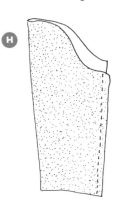

3. Set sleeve by first aligning side seam to underarm seam, RST. Wrap back dress shoulder extension around sleeve first, then front shoulder extension. Pin sleeve in place, matching notches (I). Sew. Finish seam allowances.

4. Repeat for remaining sleeve.

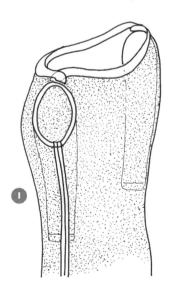

FINISH SLEEVES

1. Place two cuff pieces WST. Baste or pin top curved edge together. (J)

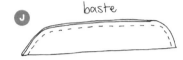

baste

2. Apply bias tape to the curved cuff edge, as you did with the neckline. (K)

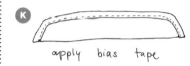

apply bias tape

3. With sleeve wrong side out. Pre-assemble the cuff overlap by matching outer notches along raw edge. Baste together. Be sure the overlap of one pre-assembled cuff is going in the opposite direction. Pin cuff to the wrong side of the sleeve, matching cuff center notch to sleeve center notch. Sew. Serge or zig-zag stitch to finish the seam allowance. (L)

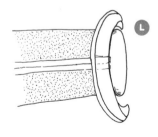

4. Edge stitch the seam allowance to the sleeve, not the cuff. Turn sleeve and dress right side out. Flip cuff to right side of the sleeve. Tack at the underarm seam. (M)

5. Repeat for remaining cuff and sleeve.

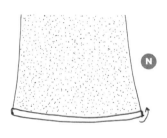

HEM

1. Hem dress by turning WST by ½" then again by ½" (N). Press and sew into place and it's ready to wear!

a

b

FLIP-FLOPS

Crazy to sew your own shoes? Never! Who cares as long as you can make them using your favorite fabrics! This would be a great gift for your bridesmaids or even a new mom. Something cute and comfy to slip on your feet is a must. This is a fun, small project not only to practice using bias tape, but also to get used to applying it to a curve.

style tips

▸ Try using a small-scale print for either the foot bed or bias tape. Any combination of solids or even chambray would be stunning too!

▸ Making a gift? Spend time thinking about your recipient's style. The prints you choose will make her (or him!) feel even more special.

MATERIALS

1 fat quarter quilting cotton for the foot bed

¼ yard cotton canvas for the sole

½ yard 20" wide heavyweight double-sided fusible ultra firm interfacing (Pellon 71F)

2¾ yards ½" wide double fold bias tape OR an additional ½ yard of quilting cotton if you are making your own (see page 62 for making bias tape)

walking foot sewing machine attachment

buttonhole foot sewing machine attachment

⅝" button for use with buttonhole foot

water-soluble pen

tracing paper

CUTTING

See pullout for pattern pieces. Trace and cut the pieces for your desired size.

From quilting cotton and canvas, cut:

(1) Flip-Flop Pattern for the left foot bed

(1) Flip-Flop Pattern mirror image for the right foot bed

From interfacings, cut:

(2) Flip-Flop Patterns for the left foot bed

(2) Flip-Flop Patterns mirror image for the right foot bed

SEAM ALLOWANCE

½" unless otherwise noted

FINISHED SIZE

Women's size 5/6, 7/8, 9/10

TIP: *You can also use a non-slip fabric, sometimes called "slipper gripper," for the sole of each flip-flop. If you do, though, I recommend that the flip-flops be used only indoors, whereas the canvas bottom should be durable enough for light/occasional outdoor wear.*

instructions

Transfer all markings from pattern pieces.

ASSEMBLE FOOT BED

1. Fuse interfacing to foot bed. Repeat for additional interfacing — making a double layer. Mark placement for buttonhole, or adjust to fit your foot. Sew ⅝" buttonhole. (A)

TIP: *Because the interfacing is double sided you might find that the heat from your iron fuses the interfacing to your ironing board during this step. If so, grab some parchment paper and layer it between the interfacing and ironing board — no more sticking!*

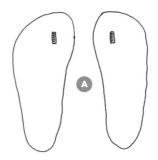

HOW TO SEW A BUTTONHOLE

Never sewn a buttonhole before? It's pretty painless actually. I recommend practicing on scrap fabric first though. It's helpful to consult your sewing machine manual too.

Most machines come with a buttonhole foot attachment. There's usually a designated spot within the foot to place the button you're using (which determines the opening size of the buttonhole). Simply mark the placement of your buttonhole and let your machine do the rest.

If your machine doesn't have the capability of automatically sewing a buttonhole, don't worry! There are only a few steps to master. First, measure the width of your button to determine the size buttonhole you'll need to make.

With a water-soluble pen, mark the buttonhole center placement. Sew a rectangle around this marked line with a small stitch length. Next, using a narrow zig-zag stitch, sew along both long sides of the rectangle over the straight stitching you made previously. Stitches should not overlap along the straight stitch. Finish by sewing a bar tack at both the top and bottom of the buttonhole. Insert a pin perpendicular to top of the buttonhole and use a seam ripper to open the buttonhole, stopping when you reach the pin. And you're done! Pretty great, right?

MAKE STRAPS

1. Cut two pieces of bias tape for straps, both approximately 10" long each. Edge stitch along both long sides of both pieces of bias tape.

2. Slip straps through the buttonhole until they reach each outer side of the base. (B)

3. With both bias tape lengths RST, use a water-soluble pen to mark where the two tapes emerge from the buttonhole.

4. Transfer strap placement lines from the pattern and ensure that the length of the tape comfortably reaches each side of the foot bed strap placement line. (B)

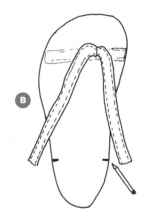

5. Remove straps from the buttonhole and stitch along marked line from Step 3, to sew bias tapes together. Reinforce with extra stitching. Approximately 1" up from that stitch line, stitch the bias tape together again. (C)

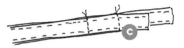

6. Slip straps back through the buttonhole just to the lower sewn line. (D)

7. Baste bias tape ends in place along edges of foot bed using a ¼" seam allowance. (E)

bottom

8. Try on flip-flops, adjusting the unsecured ends of the bias tape straps to comfortably go over your foot using the respective strap markings on each side of the foot bed as a guide. Sew in place on the bottom of the foot bed using a ¼" seam allowance and reinforce with extra stitches. (F)

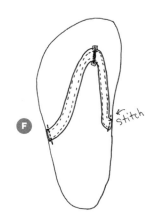

FINISH

1. Fuse canvas to bottom of foot bed. The canvas will fuse to the existing second side of the interfacing that was attached in *Assemble Foot Bed* (see page 68).

2. Open up the folded bias tape, fold, and press short end ½" to the wrong side. Starting with this end, place bias tape RST along outer edge of foot bed aligning the raw edges. Using a walking foot attachment, and following the first crease in the bias tape, sew around the entire foot bed, trying not to allow the bias tape to pucker around the curves. (G)

3. When you reach the folded end of the bias tape, continue sewing, overlapping by ½". Cut off excess bias tape. Wrap bias tape to top of the foot bed, re-fold the tape over so the raw edge is enclosed. Trim the seam allowances around the tight curves if necessary so that the tape completely covers the previous stitching.

4. With the top of the flip-flop facing up, sew into place along the inner edge of the bias tape. Use an iron to help shape the bias tape around the curves of the foot bed as necessary. Now you have some comfy, custom footwear!

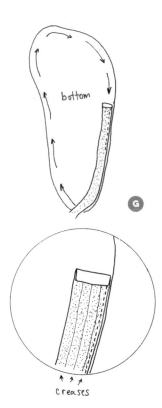

WOMEN'S TUNIC

You'll feel great all day long in this classic tunic. Great for summer days at the office, or perfectly cool and comfy at the park. The front button placket makes it easy to wear, and the drawstring waist flatters any figure. The dolman-style sleeve with cuff makes it look put together no matter what you wear it with.

style tips

▸ Choose a bold graphic or floral print to make this tunic the focal point of your outfit.

▸ Pair with leggings or skinny jeans for a casual carefree look and ultimate comfort.

MATERIALS

Lightweight fabric with a good drape (see Tip), cut:

Using 58" wide fabric:

XS-M 2⅔ yards, L-2XL 2⅞ yards

Using 45" wide fabric:

XS-M 3⅓ yards, L-2XL 3 yards

(5) ½" buttons

buttonhole foot sewing machine attachment

tracing paper (Pellon 830)

¼ yard lightweight fusible interfacing (Pellon PLF36)

TIP: *For fabric, I suggest a lawn, voile, shot cotton, chambray, or rayon. A knit would work as well, but I suggest selecting a size down. Cut the main pieces on the bias for an even softer drape — just be aware that you'll need more fabric to do so.*

CUTTING

See pullout for pattern pieces (see page 143) for cutting diagram and size chart (see page 140). Trace and cut the pieces for your desired size.

(1) Tunic front

(1) Tunic back

(1) Placket

(1) Casing

(2) Cuffs

(2) Drawstrings, cut rectangles 2" tall by 34" long for XS, 36" for S, 38" for M, 41" for L, 43" for XL, or 45" for XXL

2" wide bias cut strips, joined if necessary for a total of 1 yard — make into ½" wide double fold bias tape for neckline (see page 62)

2" wide bias cut strips, joined for a total of 2 yards — make into 1" wide single fold bias tape for hem (see page 62)

SEAM ALLOWANCE

½" unless otherwise noted

FINISHED SIZE

XS–2XL

instructions

Transfer all markings from pattern pieces.

SEW SHOULDER SEAMS

1. Matching notches, sew front to back at shoulder seams RST.

2. Finish seam allowance (see page 67). Press seams toward back of garment.

ATTACH BIAS TAPE

1. Unfold the double fold bias tape and attach to tunic neckline RST beginning at center front of neckline. Sew along first crease of bias tape around entire neckline (A), stopping at center front. Short ends of bias trim should be just touching, not overlapping. Trim excess bias tape that extends past center front.

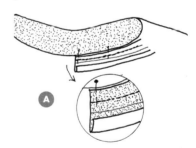

2. Fold bias tape over raw edge and pin into place. From garment front, topstitch close to the inner fold of the bias tape around neckline, being sure to catch the bias tape on the reverse side as well. (B)

3. Turn tunic wrong side out.

MAKE BUTTON PLACKET

1. Press tunic front in half to find center. Press placket in half lengthwise to find center. Place placket piece centered right side down on wrong side of center of tunic front. Placket will be placed ½" above finished bias tape neckline. Pin into place. (C)

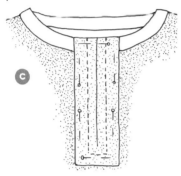

2. On placket, mark a rectangle as indicated on pattern piece.

3. Cut (2) 1" wide strips of fusible interfacing the height of the marked rectangle. Fuse to wrong side of placket piece on either side of marked rectangle.

4. Sew through both placket and tunic front following the marked lines. Cut down center of rectangle through all layers, stopping ½" from short end of rectangle and angle out to each corner of the stitching. Do not clip through stitching. Trim seam allowance inside sewn rectangle to ¼". Turn garment right side out.

5. Flip placket toward right side of garment. Press long sides of placket to the wrong side by ¼". Press seam allowance

toward placket and press top placket edges to wrong side by ½" (D). Press each folded side of placket in half, wrong sides touching, to cover stitching on rectangle from previous step. Pin. Finished placket width will measure 1".

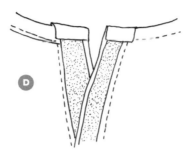

6. Topstitch along inner long edge of placket on left, folding garment out of the way. Topstitch along both long and top edges of placket on right as far as you can sew slightly longer than the sewn rectangle length from Step 2. There is now a right and left side of placket. With the placket facing you, fold the placket on left on top of the placket on right. (E)

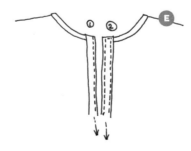

7. Trim off underside of right placket as much as you can to reduce bulk. Turn bottom of placket under by 1" to enclose all raw edges. Press and pin place.

8. From top edge of left placket piece, topstitch along top edge of placket down to the bottom, pivoting at corner, and finish by sewing a small rectangle at base of placket (F). Press.

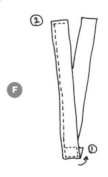

9. The buttonhole placement will vary based on the size pattern you selected. Mark top buttonhole centered on the placket, ½" from the top edge. Mark the bottom buttonhole 2½" from bottom edge of placket. Mark remaining buttonholes equidistance between top and bottom buttonholes. Create buttonholes on top placket piece at each of the markings (see page 69 for buttonhole instructions). Align and sew buttons to corresponding locations on bottom placket.

SEW SIDE SEAMS

1. Matching notches, sew front to back from the bottom of the armhole to the bottom of the dress along the side seams RST. Finish seam allowance (see page 67).

2. Press seams toward back of garment.

MAKE CUFFS

1. Take one cuff piece and fold in half widthwise RST. Sew along short end thus making a loop. Press seam open.

2. Fold cuff loop wrong sides together aligning raw edges and seam. Baste raw edges of cuff together using a scant seam allowance. With tunic wrong side out, align raw edge of cuff to raw edge of sleeve, aligning the side seam to the cuff seam. Pin in place. Sew. Serge (or zig-zag stitch) to finish the seam allowance. (G)

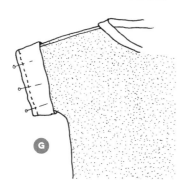

3. Turn tunic right side out and press seam allowance toward cuff. Edge stitch the seam allowance to the cuff. Fold cuff up in half, covering the seam by approximately ½". Tack cuff in place at shoulder and underarm seams. Press.

4. Repeat for remaining cuff.

MAKE WAISTBAND CASING

1. Press long edges of casing to the wrong side by ½". Fold short ends of casing to wrong sides by ½". Topstitch along both short folded edges. (H)

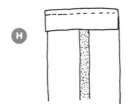

2. Align casing with transferred pattern markings and pin it to the right side of the tunic (or adjust placement as desired). Pin casing in place at indicated marking on pattern pieces or adjust placement as desired. Sew along top and bottom edges of casing, remembering to backstitch at both beginnings and ends. (I)

PREPARE DRAWSTRING

1. Sew drawstring pieces RST at one short end. Press the seam open.

2. Press short edges of drawstring to the wrong side by ½". Press in half widthwise. Open and press raw edges to center crease. Fold in half again enclosing the raw edges in the fold and press. Sew along the long open edge to finish.

3. Using a safety pin attached to one end of the drawstring, thread the drawstring through the casing.

HEM

1. Using 1" wide single fold bias tape, open up tape and press one short end of bias tape to the wrong side by ½".

2. Align short folded edge of bias tape to one side seam with bias tape RST with right side of tunic. Sew along first crease of bias tape around entire hem, overlapping when you reach the folded edge of where you began applying bias tape. Trim off any excess bias tape.

3. Press bias tape away from garment. Refold tape toward wrong side of tunic so it is completely inside garment and no raw edges are showing. Sew in place using a longer stitch length (3.0mm) along inner folded edge. Press to finish the newest addition to your wardrobe!

METAL BRACELETS

Do you have a pack of grommets or rivets lying around? Not quite sure what to do with them? Maybe you're looking to gain some new skills and want a small project to try. By choosing a variety of metal types and fabrics, you can make super-cute bracelets and have fun in the process. Why not invite some friends over and have a bracelet-making party?

style tips

▶ Having a variety of different metal rivets and grommets gives you an opportunity to play around with your favorites.

▶ Shop Etsy for jewelry findings to match the rivets or grommets.

▶ Stack a few bracelets in both sizes for a fun and layered bohemian look.

MATERIALS
Approximately 3" x 8" rectangle quilting cotton fabric adjusting length depending on desired fit (see Tip)

8mm rivets or grommets (inside diameter ⁵⁄₁₆", outside ½")

bracelet closure: 13mm ribbon ends and coordinating lobster clasps and jump rings, or 20mm leather end caps or ribbon/cording/scrap leather

strong glue such as E6000

water-soluble pen

CUTTING
All measurements are height x width.

From fabric, cut:
   (1) 3" x 6¼" rectangle for grommet bracelet OR

   (1) 1¾" x 6½" rectangle for rivet bracelet

TIP: The bracelets are designed to fit an average woman's wrist. To adjust the size, measure the wearer's wrist, subtract the amount of length the jewelry hardware adds, then add approximately ½" to the length of the quilting cotton.

instructions

PREPARE BRACELET FABRIC

1. Press quilting fabric WST in half lengthwise. Open up and press long raw edges to meet at the fold line. Fold in half along length again so that the raw edges are enclosed in the fold (A) and press.

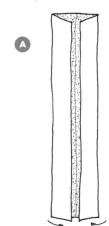

2. If you will be using jewelry closure hardware, edge stitch along the two long sides of the folded fabric. (B)

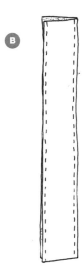

3. If you won't be using jewelry hardware, unfold the fabric, then fold the short sides in by ¼", refold and press. (C)

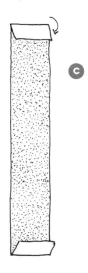

4. Tuck ribbon, cording or scrap leather into each short end of the bracelet and edge stitch along all four sides of the folded fabric. (D)

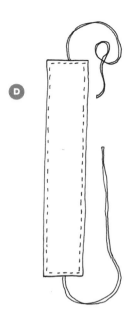

INSERT RIVETS OR GROMMETS

1. Install rivets or grommets, adjusting spacing as desired (see Sidebar).

2. If you are using closure hardware, insert raw ends of bracelets into hardware and secure with glue before clamping the hardware. (E)

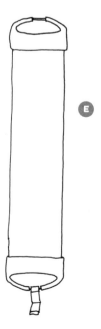

INSTALLING RIVETS AND GROMMETS

Installing rivets and grommets might seem a little intimidating at first, but these bracelets are a fast, fun, and easy way to give them a try. Most rivet sets and grommet sets come with some instructions for installing. Here is a general outline of the steps and materials you'll be using:

Rivets

Mark placement of rivet with water-soluble pen. Using either a leather hole punch or very sharp scissors, make a small hole to insert the part of the rivet with the post. Be sure the hole is just a bit smaller than the rivet post. If the hole you cut is too big, the rivet might not install correctly or the fabric may fray. With the back side of the project facing you, insert rivet post down into the hole. Flipping over to the front, slip the cap end of the rivet over the post. Using the anvil and strike plate that came with your rivet set, layer the strike plate, then top of rivet, then anvil. Secure by hitting anvil with rubber mallet or hammer.

Grommets

Inserting a grommet is similar to installing a rivet. Most grommets at a craft supply store either come with or refer to, a grommet setting tool for setting that particular size. Again, mark and make a hole for your size grommet by tracing the inner diameter of grommet with a water-soluble pen. Insert grommet post through the front side of the project, flip project over, and place grommet washer over grommet. Use the strike plate and anvil to set grommet in place.

Another option

You can also purchase a rivet/grommet press. These presses are fairly expensive (especially compared to a basic setting tool you can get at a craft store) but can be worth the investment if you plan to install lots of rivets or grommets.

ZIP TOP TOTE

A great bag to tote around anywhere: the beach, the farmers market or the store. It holds your gear in style and there's even a hidden pocket for your keys, sunglasses, or lip balm. An interior zipper will keep important things secure, and the zip top makes it easy to throw the tote in your car and go. Feature a favorite large-scale print you've been holding on to.

style tips

▶ Leather straps are nothing to fear! If you prefer fabric straps, cut (2) 4" x 25" straps and construct in the same way as the Bucket Bag project strap (see page 88).

▶ Rivets in the top corners of the hidden pocket add a great detail as well as reinforcing the pocket opening.

MATERIALS

¼ yard top exterior (home dec, denim, canvas, or heavy linen, 54" wide)

½ yard hidden pocket exterior (home dec, denim, canvas, or heavy linen, 54" wide)

¾ yard hidden pocket lining (quilting cotton)

1 yard lining (quilting cotton)

1¾ yards 20" wide woven fusible interfacing (Pellon SF101)

18" x 58" package ByAnnie's Soft and Stable stabilizer, or 1 yard cotton canvas (see page 79 for information on using canvas as a stabilizer)

22" non-separating zipper

11" non-separating zipper

water-soluble pen

(2) 1" x 25" leather straps

zipper foot sewing machine attachment

denim sewing machine needle/ size #16

CUTTING

All measurements are height x width.

From tote exterior fabric, cut:
(2) 6" x 22" rectangles

From hidden pocket exterior, cut:
(2) 14" x 22" rectangles

From hidden pocket lining fabric, cut:
(2) 12" x 22" rectangles

From lining fabric, cut:
(2) 17" x 22" rectangles

(1) 2" x 3¼" rectangle for zipper end tab

(2) 13" x 15" rectangles

From interfacing, cut:
(2) 17" x 22" rectangles

(1) 13" x 15" rectangle

From stabilizer, cut:
(2) 17" x 22" rectangles

SEAM ALLOWANCE

½" unless otherwise noted

FINISHED SIZE

13" tall x 21" wide x 6" deep

TIP: *Having a hard time locating leather straps? Try using upcycled leather belts from a second hand store. Just make sure the leather is thin enough to sew through. No luck at the thrift shop? Etsy is a great resource for finished straps.*

instructions

HIDDEN POCKET

1. Hem exterior hidden pocket by folding over the top edge ¼" to the wrong side, press. Fold over again 1". Press.

2. Secure hem in place by sewing close to inner fold. Edge stitch top of hidden pocket. (A)

3. Repeat for remaining exterior hidden pocket.

ASSEMBLE EXTERIOR

1. Place tote exterior panel and hidden pocket lining RST along 22" length. Pin and sew along the long edge. Repeat for remaining tote exterior panel and hidden pocket lining. Press seam allowance toward the lining. (B)

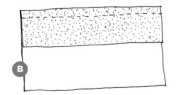

2. Place exterior hidden pocket wrong side down on right side of assembled exterior, aligning and pinning along the bottom and side raw edges. On exterior hidden pocket, mark a 8" x 6" rectangle in the center of the panel. Starting at bag edge, topstitch on hidden pocket along previous topstitching to top left of marked rectangle (do a few backstitches at the corner for reinforcement), then stitch down the left, across the bottom, up the right side of the marked rectangle, and finally over to the right raw edge of the bag (C). Repeat for other exterior pocket and assembled exterior. You will now have two assembled panels that are the front and back of the tote, each measuring 17" x 22".

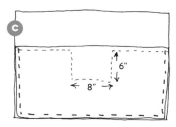

3. Baste assembled exterior to stabilizer along outer edge using a scant seam allowance.

4. On exterior panel, mark center by folding in half and finger pressing. Baste strap 3½" from each side of this mark, aligning inside edge of strap to each mark (D). Be sure not to create a twist in the handle.

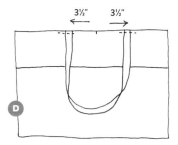

5. Repeat for second strap and remaining assembled exterior piece. Set aside.

> **TIP:** *Don't be too concerned about sewing through the leather handles in this step. It's a good idea to use 100% polyester or 100% nylon upholstery weight thread when sewing anything with leather — all-cotton thread will deteriorate with age.*

INSTALL ZIPPERED INTERIOR POCKET

1. Fuse interfacing to wrong side of one zip pocket lining piece and both lining pieces. Center the 15" edge of zip pocket piece on the bag lining RST, aligning to top long raw edge of lining. With a water-soluble pen, mark a rectangle 4½" down from top edge of pocket lining piece, centered, 11¼" wide by ½" tall. Sew around the entire rectangle, following the marked line.

2. Cut through both layers of fabric down the center of the rectangle and angling out to corners at each end (E). Be sure not to clip through stitching, but right up to it. Pull the pocket lining through the cut opening so that fabrics are WST. Press.

> **TIP:** *This part can be a little tricky, especially if it's your first time. It helps to finger press at first and follow up with a good press.*

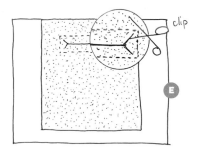

3. With bag lining piece right side up, place 11" zipper behind the opening, ensuring that zipper pull is within the opening, and pin in place or use ¼" fusible tape to temporarily hold it in place. With a zipper foot, topstitch along edge of opening around the whole rectangle to securely attach the zipper. (F)

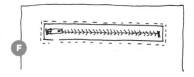

4. Turn bag lining over so that it is right side down. Take the remaining second pocket lining piece and place it right side down on the pocket lining piece you have just sewn. Pocket pieces will be RST. Pin through both pocket lining pieces (but not through to bag lining piece) and sew along sides and bottom of the pocket lining. Baste along top raw edge through all layers. Set aside.

PREPARE AND INSTALL TOP ZIPPER

1. At pull side of zipper, bend each zipper tape end back on itself by 45 degrees, baste or hand stitch in place. (G)

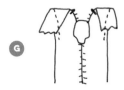

2. Press zipper tab in half RST widthwise. Press both short edges WST by ½". Sew along both raw edges, backstitching at both ends. Clip corners. (H)

3. Turn right side out and slip over zipper end tape. Press and topstitch around all four edges of the tab. (I)

4. Lay one assembled exterior panel right side up. Place 22" zipper (teeth side down) on top with the zipper pull at the left, aligning the long zipper tape edge to the top raw edge of the exterior panel. Make sure that the metal stop near the zipper pull is ¾" away from the left edge of the exterior panel. Layer bag lining piece without the zippered pocket (right side facing down) on top of zipper. Pin and baste using a scant seam allowance to keep the layers from shifting in the next step. (J)

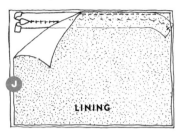

5. Using your zipper foot, sew using a ¼" seam allowance. Stopping 1½" before the edge of the fabric, backstitch and pull the zipper tape away from the seam removing any basting stitches to do so, bending it down out of the way, in toward the fabric. Keep fabric edges aligned and continue stitching along until you reach the edge.

6. Position fabrics WST and press along zipper tape.

> **TIP:** *Do not topstitch along either side of the zipper at this point. We'll be doing that in another step toward the end.*

7. Lay second exterior panel right side up. Place zipper (with fabrics attached) on top, teeth side down and with the zipper pull at the right. Exterior fabrics will be RST. Make sure the metal stop near zipper pull is ¾" away from the right edge of the exterior panel. Lay bag lining piece on top, RST. Pin, then baste using a scant seam allowance. (K)

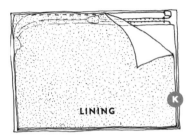

8. Using your zipper foot, sew using a ¼" seam allowance. Stopping 1½" before the edge of the fabric, backstitch and pull the zipper tape away from the seam removing any basting stitches to do so. Bend it down out of the way, in toward the fabric. Keep fabric edges aligned and continue stitching along until you reach the edge.

9. Position fabrics WST and press well along zipper.

SELECTING INTERFACING AND STABILIZERS

If you haven't used a variety of interfacings before, you might find it difficult to determine which kind you'll prefer for each project. I believe that interfacing is half personal preference and half experience. Each project calls for a specific kind of interfacing or combination of interfacings, but feel free to change these to suit your needs and style preference.

I've recommended using either ByAnnie's Soft and Stable or cotton canvas as a stabilizing interfacing for this project. If your preference is to have a bag that is sturdy, structured, and stands up on its own when empty, the Soft and Stable is your best bet. It's a great product that will provide structure and stability, and it's still easy to sew with. On the other hand, if you want a soft yet durable bag, I'd recommend using cotton canvas as interfacing. Cotton canvas moves with your exterior fabric. The bag will be sturdy but slouchy when not full.

Fabric choices also play an extremely important role in selecting the type of interfacing you'll need. For instance, if you have your heart set on using your favorite quilting cotton print in this project, extra interfacing will be needed. My favorite interfacing is a woven fusible that works really well when combined with quilting cottons. It's almost like upgrading your fabric to a home dec weight.

10. Position exterior panels RST and bag linings RST (the zipper and handles will be hidden in the middle). Open the zipper a few inches. Pin around perimeter, matching side seams for hidden pockets on exterior. Sew around all edges, leaving an opening approximately 6" wide in the bottom or one side of the bag lining. (L)

> **TIP:** *Get within ¼" of the metal zipper ends on pull side, and bend the zipper end down into the bag on the other side, making sure it doesn't get caught in the seam.*

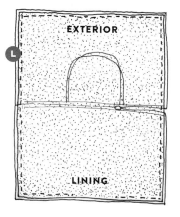

BOX CORNERS

1. Pinch each corner right sides together, aligning the side seam to bottom seam. Mark a 6" long line perpendicular to side seam 3" from the corner tip. Sew on line.

2. Trim seam allowance to ½" (M). Repeat for remaining corners (two exterior panels, and two lining pieces).

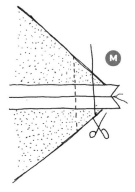

FINISH

1. Pull bag right side out through the 6" opening from Step 10. Tuck in raw edges of opening and pin. Sew the opening closed by machine using a scant seam allowance. Push lining into assembled exterior.

2. Press around entire opening and carefully along the zipper. With zipper fully open, topstitch around the complete opening of the bag using a slightly longer stitch length, taking your time to ensure a neat finish to your new bag. (N)

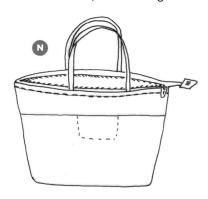

TABLET CASE

This small portfolio case is a perfect place to tuck in your tablet or reader and a notebook or calendar. The back pocket is great for corralling small notes or receipts, and the tiny front pocket is just the right size to stash some ear buds or screen wipes. You'll love bringing this along to your favorite coffee shop or to your next meeting.

style tips

▶ Using coordinating metals for the zipper and snap really makes the case look professionally assembled.

▶ Consider quilting the main pieces before assembly.

MATERIALS

½ yard quilting cotton or home dec fabric for the exterior

½ yard quilting cotton for the lining

scraps of quilting cotton for the tiny pocket and pocket lining

½ yard 20" wide woven fusible interfacing (Pellon SF101)

½ yard 45" wide fusible fleece (Pellon 987F)

½ yard ½" wide bias tape piping (see page 62 to make your own)

1 yard ½" wide double fold bias tape (see page 62 to make your own)

11" non-separating zipper

size 24 metal snap

zipper foot sewing machine attachment

walking foot sewing machine attachment (optional)

tracing paper

snap setter

CUTTING

See pullout for pattern pieces. Trace and cut the required pieces.

All measurements are height x width.

From exterior fabric, cut:
(2) Main exterior

(1) Back Pocket

From lining, cut:
(2) Main exterior

(1) Back Pocket

From scraps of quilting cotton, cut:
(1) Tiny Pocket

(1) Tiny Pocket lining

From fusible fleece, cut:
(2) Main exterior

From interfacing, cut:
(1) Back Pocket

(1) Tiny Pocket

SEAM ALLOWANCE
½" unless otherwise noted

FINISHED SIZE
9½" tall x 13" wide x 1½" deep

instructions

Transfer all markings from the pattern pieces.

ATTACH FUSIBLE FLEECE AND INTERFACING

1. Fuse fleece to wrong side of main exterior pieces.

2. Fuse interfacing to wrong side of back pocket exterior piece and tiny exterior pocket piece.

MAKE DARTS

1. Transfer darts onto wrong side of both main exterior, back exterior pocket, main lining and back pocket lining pieces.

2. Align dart legs so that the fabric is RST. Sew along dart leg, backstitching at innermost point. (A)

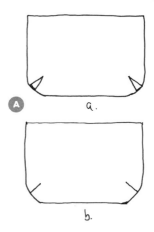

3. Press dart outward on exterior fabrics and inward on lining fabrics.

MAKE TINY POCKET

1. Place tiny pocket pieces RST. Sew along curved edge (B). Notch curve. Turn right side out. Press.

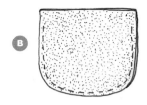

2. Cut a 5" length of ½" wide double fold binding. Refold in half lengthwise RST (C). Sew along both short ends.

3. Trim seam allowance to ¼". Turn so that the binding is right side out. Press. Slip over top edge of pocket. Edge stitch along bottom folded edge being sure to catch the binding on the reverse side as well. (D)

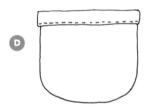

4. Place tiny pocket as marked on front exterior. Topstitch in place around sides and bottom (not the top), reinforcing at both top corners as indicated. (E)

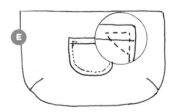

MAKE BACK POCKET
1. Baste piping to top edge of the right side of the back pocket, raw edges aligned, using a ¼" seam allowance.

2. Place back pocket lining RST. Sew along edge following piping, using zipper foot to get in close to piping (F). Position pieces WST. Press.

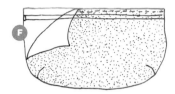

3. Topstitch across top of back pocket just below piping. (G)

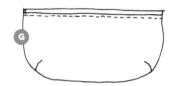

4. Place back pocket right side up on back exterior. Align to bottom and sides of back exterior. Both exteriors will be face up. Baste using a ¼" seam allowance. (H)

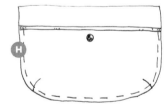

5. Following the manufacturer's instructions, install snap (refer to pattern piece for placement).

ASSEMBLE
1. Trim zipper tape at each end to ½" past metal end stops.

2. Lay main exterior with pocket right side up. Place zipper, left side down on top edge, aligning zipper tape to top raw edge. With the zipper pull at the left, place lining right side down on top (I). Use your zipper foot to sew along zipper tape edge using a ¼" seam allowance.

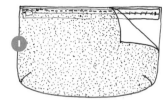

3. Position pieces WST. Press fabrics away from zipper teeth.

4. Repeat Steps 1 and 2 for the other side of the zipper. Be sure that both sides of the case are in line with each other. From bottom to top, layers will be:

1. Remaining exterior right side up.

2. Finished unit from Step 2 exterior face down with zipper tape aligned to the top raw edge.

3. Remaining lining right side down on top.

5. Topstitch along both sides of zipper. (J)

6. Fold in half so that the lining pieces are RST with the zipper at top. Pin and baste in place using a ¼" seam allowance along sides and bottom. (K)

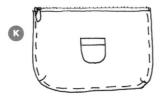

APPLY BIAS TAPE

1. Working from the back, unfold bias tape and place right side down on top of the case. Align raw edges to case sides. Trim tape so it extends ½" above both top case edges. Sew along first crease through all layers (L). Press bias tape away from project.

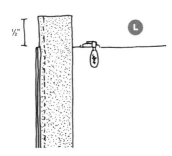

2. At top corners, fold bias tape over top edge, pin or hold in place (M). Refold bias tape to front of case, wrapping to cover raw edge and just covering the previous stitching line. Pin.

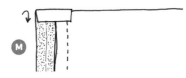

3. Topstitch close to the inner fold of binding, backstitching at both the beginning and end.

VARIATION: PENCIL CASE

Always searching in your bag for a pencil or a pen? This companion case will keep them tucked in your backpack or bag. Perfect for students and adults alike, this simple pencil case is great for gifting. It's also an ideal project for a new sewist to get experience installing a zipper and working with bias tape.

style tips

▶ Consider using pieced patchwork or improv piecing for the exterior pieces or embellish them with some hand stitching or embroidery. Either (or both!) can truly personalize this case.

▶ If you want to use scrappy bias tape, join 3-4" long pieces of 2" wide bias strips until you have one yard total — it's a great way to show off those precious scraps you've been saving. Using a solid fabric for the exterior pieces will make the case pop!

MATERIALS

¼ yard quilting cotton for the exterior

¼ yard quilting cotton for the lining

½ yard fusible woven interfacing

¾ yard ½" wide double fold bias tape (or see page 62 to make your own)

8" non-separating zipper

CUTTING

See pullout for pattern pieces. Trace and cut the required pieces.

From exterior fabric, lining fabric, and fusible interfacing, cut:

(2) Main Pencil Case

SEAM ALLOWANCE

½" unless otherwise noted

FINISHED SIZE

5" x 9½"

instructions

Transfer all markings from the pattern pieces.

ASSEMBLE

Follow the instructions for the Tablet Case to assemble. There are no darts for this project, nor are there any pockets. Otherwise, the assembly is the same.

MARKET BAG

Reminiscent of a vintage rattan picnic bag, this quilted version is a classic shape that you'll love. The bag has a casual yet sophisticated look that will work with any outfit and carry all you need. A handy zippered compartment secures keys or spare change, and leather straps add beauty and durability.

style tips

▸ Using muted or bright colors can really change the feel of this bag. Muted gives a more calm and natural look, whereas brights really pop! Scraps would be fun too. Express yourself!

MATERIALS

1 yard quilting cotton for the exterior

1 yard quilting cotton for the lining

1 fat eighth quilting cotton for inside pocket

Strips: A variety of 2½" wide scraps of various lengths (totaling approximately 4 yards)

1¾ yard 20" wide fusible woven interfacing (Pellon SF101)

18" x 58" package ByAnnie's Soft and Stable stabilizer

5" non-separating zipper

(2) 1" x 16" leather straps

upholstery-weight coordinating polyester or nylon thread (for attaching handles)

zipper foot sewing machine attachment

walking foot sewing machine attachment

leather sewing machine needle

tracing paper

water-soluble pen

CUTTING

See pullout for pattern pieces. Trace and cut the required pieces.

All measurements are height x width.

From exterior fabric, cut:
(2) Market Bag Main Panels

(2) 2" x WOF strips for making ½" double fold straight grain binding (see page 62 to make into binding)

(1) Market Bag Base

From lining fabric, cut:
(2) Market Bag Main Panels

(1) Market Bag Base

From pocket fabric, cut:
(1) 14" x 6" rectangle for zippered interior pocket

From strip scraps, cut:
2½" wide strips of varying lengths (5-12" long) for patchwork strips

From stabilizer, cut:
(2) Market Bag Main Panels

(1) Market Bag Base

From interfacing, cut:
(2) Market Bag Main Panels
(1) Market Bag Base

SEAM ALLOWANCE

½" unless otherwise noted

FINISHED SIZE

23" wide x 12" tall x 7" deep

instructions

Transfer all markings from the pattern pieces.

MAKE EXTERIOR

1. Baste exterior main and base panels to stabilizer using a ¼" seam allowance. Mark a horizontal line 4½" down from top raw edge on exterior main panel.

2. Assemble patchwork strips to the length of main panel by sewing short ends together and pressing seams open. Repeat to make four pieced strips.

3. Place one pieced strip right side down on main panel, above and aligned to the marked line. Sew using ¼" seam allowance (A). Flip and press strip with the wrong side of the strip against the right side of the exterior.

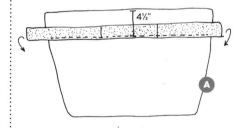

4. Repeat Step 3 with a second pieced strip by layering raw edge RST with previous strip. Sew using ¼" seam allowance. Press unsewn edge of strip to the WS by ¼" (B). Press down with the wrong side of the strip against the right side of the exterior. Topstitch along bottom folded edge of second strip to hold in place.

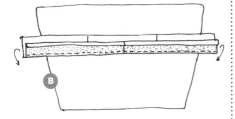

5. Repeat Steps 1–4 for second exterior main panel. Set aside.

6. Quilt panels and base using straight lines ¼" to ⅜" apart.

7. Trim excess patchwork strips flush to main panel sides.

ASSEMBLE EXTERIOR AND LINING

1. Place assembled exterior main panels RST and sew side seams (C). Press seams open.

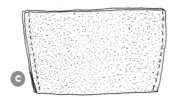

2. Mark exterior base and bottom edge of exterior main panels into quarters. To do this, fold in half lengthwise and mark on fold within seam allowance. Then fold in half widthwise and mark on fold.

3. Align main panel side seams with base end markings RST. Pin in place. Repeat for base center side markings and exterior main panels center markings. Add additional pins to secure in place . Sew with main pieces facing up to avoid pinching (D). Notch curves.

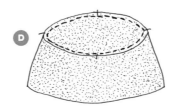

4. Turn right side out.

5. Fuse interfacing to wrong side of all corresponding lining pieces.

6. Repeat Steps 1-3 with lining main panel and base piece to create bag lining.

7. Slip lining into assembled exterior WST. Align side seams. Pin at top raw edge. Baste using ¼" seam allowance. Set aside.

MAKE DROP-DOWN ZIPPERED POCKET

1. Trim zipper tape ends to extend ½" past metal end stops on both ends.

2. Center zipper tape teeth side down on right side of the pocket fabric, aligned to raw edge of one short side (E). Pin.

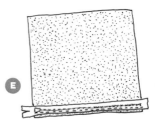

3. Sew using a zipper foot and a ¼" seam allowance. Align second short edge with the other zipper tape edge and sew along the long edge using a ¼" seam allowance. (F)

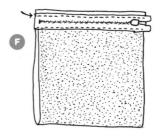

4. Turn right side out. The pocket is now the shape of a tube. Press fabric away from zipper, opening zipper for easier access. Using your zipper foot attachment, topstitch along each side of zipper. Fold pocket so zipper is 1" below the top edge. Press.

BIND SIDES AND ATTACH POCKET

1. Open up ½" double fold binding and place RST on the back of drop-down pocket, aligning raw edge of binding with raw edge of pocket side. Leave a ½" overhang at bottom. Sew along first crease of the binding. Fold bottom overhang up and wrap binding to front of pocket, refolding and covering raw edge. Sew along inner fold of binding. (G)

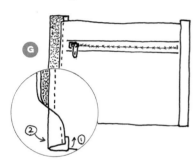

2. Repeat Step 1 to bind remaining pocket side.

3. Align the pocket with center back lining. Ensure alignment of the raw edges of bag and pocket and baste into place along the top edge using a ¼" seam, through all layers.

BIND TOP EDGE

1. Open up remaining ½" double fold binding and press one short end of binding to wrong side by ½". Working from lining side, align raw edge to top raw edge of lining panels beginning at the side seam with the folded end of the binding. Sew along first crease of binding, overlapping raw end when you reach the binding where you began.

2. Wrap binding towards bag exterior, covering raw edge and previous stitching (H). Sew in place close to the inner fold of the binding.

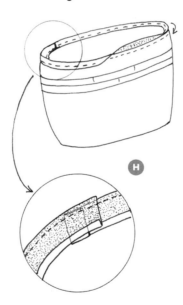

ATTACH HANDLES

1. Finger press exterior in half to find the center of tote front and back panels, and mark with a water-soluble pen. Measure 2½" from either side of center mark and again mark with a water-soluble pen. Align inner edge of each leather handle to 2½" marking and handle end 1½" from top bound edge. (I)

2. Using a denim sewing needle and coordinating polyester or nylon thread, sew a ¾" square box. Reinforce with an X through each box (J) and you are ready to grab this and go!

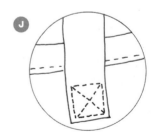

GADGET CASE

You can whip up this great little case in no time! The front pocket securely stores your phone, and you can tuck your library card, bank card, or even a few bills in the back. Toss it in your handbag or put it in your pocket to keep everything together and within easy reach.

style tips

▸ This fun little project is great for gifting! Because this gadget case is so quick to make, it's easy to sew up more than one at a time.

▸ The front pocket doesn't have to be used for a phone. Think of tucking in a small notepad instead!

MATERIALS

2 coordinating fat quarters (A and B) or ¼ yard cuts

¼ yard double-sided heavyweight fusible interfacing (such as Pellon 72F)

approximately 2¼" of ½" wide ribbon or twill tape

tracing paper

water-soluble pen

CUTTING

See pullout for pattern pieces. Trace and cut the required pieces.

All measurements are height x width.

From Fat Quarter A, cut:
(1) 6" x 4½" rectangle for front panel

(2) 5" x 4½" rectangles for pocket and pocket lining

From Fat Quarter B, cut:
(1) 17½" x 4½" rectangle for card slots

From interfacing, cut:
(1) 5¼" x 3¼" rectangle

SEAM ALLOWANCE
¼" unless otherwise noted

FINISHED SIZE
5½" x 3½"

instructions

Transfer all markings from pattern pieces.

MAKE NOTCHED POCKET

1. Place pocket pieces RST. Using pattern and a water-soluble pen, mark sewing line. Sew on drawn line, following the curve, keeping needle down and pivoting at curve corners. Trim seam allowance to ¼", clipping corners and notching curves. (A)

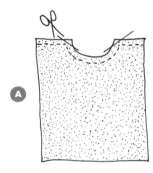

2. Position pocket pieces WST. Press. Edge stitch along top (curved) edge.

3. Place notched pocket on top of the front piece with raw edges aligned to bottom. Baste the pocket piece along both sides and bottom edge, using ⅛" seam allowance. (B)

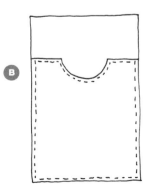

INSERT LOOP

1. Fold ribbon in half to make a loop. With raw edges aligned, place the ribbon loop in line with the top pocket edge and baste in place. Set aside.

MAKE CARD SLOTS

1. Pick one 4½" end of the card slot to be the top. From this edge, measure and mark along both long sides at 4", 7", 10½" and 13¼". Connect marked points to draw four lines across the card slot. There should be 4¼" remaining at the bottom.

2. Fold and press card slots accordion-style according to illustration (C). Be sure that finished pocket is 6" tall.

3. Edge stitch along each folded pocket edge to create two card slots (C). Baste with ⅛" seam allowance along each side to hold pockets in place.

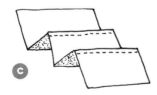

ASSEMBLE

1. Press long side edges of pocket and card slot units ½" to the wrong side. Unfold.

2. Place pocket unit RST with assembled front piece. Be sure pocket openings are both facing the same direction. Sew only the top and bottom seams, backstitching at both ends (D). Clip the corners. Turn right side out. Tuck side edges in by ½" and press.

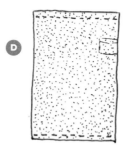

3. Slip interfacing between layers, tuck in side edges (E), and press well to fuse. Topstitch along all edges and it's ready to hold all your essentials.

BUCKET BAG

Here's my take on a classic bucket bag. It's roomy and great for on-the-go. Its cross-body adjustable strap makes this bag comfortable for a busy day of fun and adventures. Two exterior zippered pockets are an easy spot to stash your phone and keys, while the roomy interior and slip pocket will hold all your other essentials.

style tips

▸ Cotton/linen canvas blends are my favorite choice for a slouchy casual bag like this.

▸ Use color blocking to create a fun look by cutting the two exterior pieces from contrasting fabrics.

MATERIALS

½ yard canvas, twill, home dec or denim for exterior panels

1 yard quilting cotton for lining

1½ yards quilting cotton for accents

2 yards 20" wide fusible woven interfacing (Pellon SF101)

¼" wide fusible tape (optional)

(2) 5" non-separating zippers

(8) ⅜" grommets

1½" strap slider and (1) 1½" metal rectangle

cord stopper or scrap of leather (1" tall x 4" wide) for making your own

zipper foot sewing machine attachment (optional)

(2) ¼" wide x 5" long strips of leather for zipper pulls (optional)

tracing paper

water-soluble pen

CUTTING

See pullout for pattern pieces. Trace and cut the required pieces.

All measurements are height x width.

From exterior fabric, cut:
(2) 14" x 19" rectangles for main exterior

From lining fabric, cut:
(2) 14" x 19" rectangles for main lining

(1) Base

(2) 12" x 7½" rectangles for zippered pockets

(2) 7" squares for slip pocket

From accent fabric, cut:
(1) Base

(4) 3½" x 18" rectangles for top bands

(2) 6" x 31" strips for long strap

(1) 6" square for short strap

(1) 2" x 44" drawcord

From interfacing, cut:
(2) 14" x 19" rectangles for main exterior

(1) Base

(2) 3½" x 18" rectangles for top bands

(3) 6" x 20" rectangles for long strap

(1) 6" square for short strap

SEAM ALLOWANCE
½" unless otherwise noted

FINISHED SIZE
15½" tall x 13" wide x 9" deep

instructions

Transfer all markings from pattern pieces.

FUSE INTERFACING

Fuse interfacing to all corresponding exterior and accent fabrics except for the two long strap pieces. Two top bands will not have interfacing.

MAKE STRAP

1. Sew two long strap pieces RST along the short edge. Press seam open. On wrong side of fabric, fuse long strap interfacing end to end to cover length of strap fabric.

2. Press long strap in half lengthwise. Open and align long raw edges to center fold line. Press. Fold in half again and press. Topstitch along both long edges. Add additional rows of topstitching as desired. Finish short raw edges with zig-zag stitch if you prefer. Set aside.

3. Repeat Step 2 for short strap. Loop through metal rectangle. Baste raw edges together. Set aside.

4. Take one end of long strap piece and loop over middle bar of strap slider piece. Fold strap over so it bends back on itself by 2". Sew in place. (A)

5. Take opposite long strap end, thread through the short strap piece rectangular hardware, and loop it up and over the center bar of the slider hardware piece and back down the other side (B). Set the finished strap aside.

ASSEMBLE EXTERIOR

1. On wrong side of the short edge of the zippered pocket lining, centered 1½" below top raw edge, mark a rectangle 5¼" wide by ½" tall. With main exterior facing right side up, layer marked zippered pocket lining on top, RST, 3½" down from top edge and aligned with side raw edge. Sew along marked rectangle through both layers. Use sharp scissors to clip through both layers down the center of the sewn rectangle, angling out to the corners at each end of the rectangle. Take care to not clip into any stitches. (C)

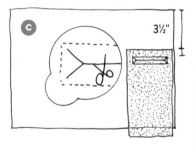

2. Pull pocket lining through rectangle to the back. Fabrics should now be WST. Press carefully around the opening to get a nice crisp edge.

3. Place zipper behind opening. Pin or use ¼" fusible tape to temporarily hold the zipper in place. Topstitch around rectangle to secure zipper. (D)

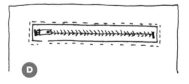

4. With wrong side of main exterior facing up, fold bottom edge of zippered pocket lining up in half to meet the top edge of pocket lining RST. Pin and sew through only the zippered pocket fabric (not the main). Sew along top and the right side of the pocket. Baste through all layers (the folded zippered pocket and the main) of the left raw pocket edge using a ¼" seam allowance. (E)

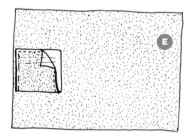

5. Repeat Steps 1–4 for the remaining zipper pocket and main exterior panel, aligning but mirroring, the zipper placement and assembly (F).

6. Place main exterior pieces RST. Sew along side seam. Press seam open. From the front exterior, topstitch on both sides of the seam. (G)

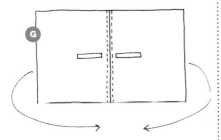

7. Repeat for the second side. These seams will be the center back and center front of the bag (H). Set aside.

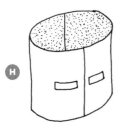

8. On the exterior main base, find the center by folding in half along the length and marking at the edge. Fold in half along the width and mark again. Repeat for bottom edge of main exterior panels using the front/back seams as a guide. (I)

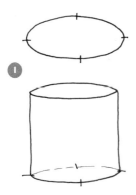

9. With RST, align the base/main quarter markings. Pin and sew in place with main exterior pieces facing up. Notch curves and set aside.

> **TIP:** *By having the main exterior pieces facing up, you can make sure you aren't accidentally sewing any wrinkles or pleats in place.*

ASSEMBLE LINING

1. Place slip pocket pieces RST and sew along all edges leaving a 4" opening at the bottom for turning. Clip corners. Turn right side out through opening. Push corners out (I use a chopstick for this). Fold the raw edges of the opening inward and press entire pocket. Topstitch along the entire top edge of pocket for a neat finish.

2. Place lining panels RST. Sew one side seam (this becomes the back seam). Press seam open. Center slip pocket on this seam, 3" down from top raw edge. Pin. Topstitch along both sides and bottom of the pocket. Reinforce pocket by sewing a small triangle at the top corner of one side of the pocket, continuing down that side, across the bottom of the pocket, up the remaining side, and finishing with another triangle. (J)

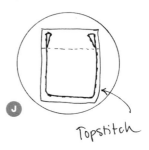

Topstitch

3. Repeat Steps 7–9 from *Assemble Exterior* section to assemble main lining.

MAKE AND ATTACH TOP BAND

1. Place two interfaced top band pieces RST and sew along both short ends. Press seams open. This will now be referred to as the exterior band. Repeat for remaining (non-interfaced) top band pieces. These will now be referred to as the lining band.

2. Aligning raw edges, center strap on side seams with strap's right side facing right side of the exterior band loop. Baste strap in place using a ¼" seam allowance being sure the strap is not twisted. (K)

> **TIP**: *Now is a great time to check that you have the strap installed correctly. If you hold the strap and let the top assembled band dangle, the strap and hardware should look correct. If not, remove the stitches and try again.*

3. Press one edge of the lining band loop WST by ½" (L). Place the lining band loop over exterior band loop, RST with raw (unfolded) edges and side seams aligned. Sew along top raw edge.

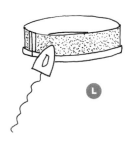

4. Position band fabrics WST. Press. Topstitch along top edge. (M)

ATTACH TOP BAND

1. Insert lining into exterior so WST. Pin together along top bag opening, matching front and back seams (N). Baste together at top edge of bag opening.

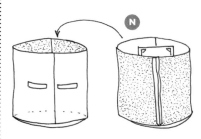

2. Take assembled main and align front and back center seams, folding in half and finger pressing (O) to find 'sides' of bag. Place a pin 3" away from either side of one 'side' marking.

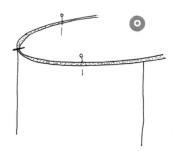

3. Between the pins, sew two rows of basting stitches: one using a ¼" seam allowance and a second using a ½" seam allowance (P). Leave long thread tails at both ends. Pull bobbin threads to gather. Repeat for remaining 'side' marking.

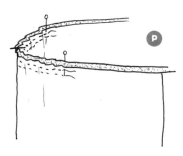

4. Unfold assembled top band.

5. Slip assembled band over bag exterior right sides together (with unfolded edge aligning to top raw edge of bag exterior). Strap will lay on outside of the bag (Q). Align side seams of band to 'side' markings on exterior. Re-pin, adjusting gathers at sides as needed to fit top band. Sew, keeping lining band down facing exterior of the bag and out of the way as you sew around the top of the bag.

6. Flip band up away from bag and press seam toward lining band. Bring lining band's folded edge down so that it covers the raw interior seam, band pieces will be WST. Pin or use fusible tape.

7. Working from exterior, topstitch along bottom edge of exterior band, being sure to catch the lining band in the seam on the interior of bag.

INSTALL GROMMETS AND MAKE DRAWCORD

1. Finger press top band in half aligning side seams and mark front and back center. Mark on top band exterior 2" away from center front and center back marking on both sides. Mark 4" away from the first set of marks. You have 8 markings in total, equally spaced around the top band. Install grommets following the instructions from the Metal Bracelets (see page 75) project. (R)

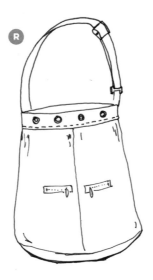

2. To make the drawcord, fold and press each short end of drawcord to the wrong side by ½". Press drawcord in half lengthwise. Open up and press long raw edges to center crease. Refold in half and press. Topstitch along open edge of drawcord. Insert cord, weaving in between grommets.

3. Insert drawcord into cord stopper or make one using a leather scrap by folding leather into a loop, overlapping by ½" or adjust to fit your drawcord. Sew down center of leather, being sure to backstitch (S). Knot ends of drawcord if desired and your classic bucket bag is complete!

MAKEUP TRAVEL CASE

I love a good travel case, something to corral all those necessities in a pretty way! Having a beautiful travel accessory makes packing fun. Elasticized slip pockets and zippered pocket compartments hold all the beauty supplies you need for any trip. This is a great project to learn a few new tricks and is suitable for a confident intermediate sewist.

style tips

▶ Patchwork on the exterior would be stunning and a beautifully customized option for this case.

▶ If you'd like to use a solid or semi-solid fabric on the outside, consider using a really fun or bright fabric for the lining.

▶ Not sure if you'll need all the pockets or feel that you prefer one style to the other? Pick and choose to create the perfect style case for you!

MATERIALS

½ yard quilting cotton for the exterior

½ yard quilting cotton for the lining

½ yard quilting cotton for the interior pockets

½ yard cotton canvas (7 oz. weight) for interfacing

⅓ yard double-sided heavyweight fusible interfacing (Pellon 72F)

⅓ yard low-loft cotton batting

30" two-way head-to-head zipper

10" non-separating zipper

2½ yards ½" wide bias piping or an additional ½ yard of quilting cotton and 2½ yards of ⅛" diameter cording if you are making your own (see page 95)

13½" of ¼" wide braided polyester elastic

2½ yards 1" wide cotton twill tape

zipper foot or piping foot sewing machine attachment

walking foot sewing machine attachment for quilting

tracing paper

water-soluble pen

CUTTING

See pullout for pattern pieces. Trace and cut the required pieces.
All measurements are height x width.

From exterior fabric, cut:
(2) front/back panels

(2) 2½" x 31½" rectangles for gusset

(1) 5¼" x 6½" rectangle for hinge

(1) 2¼" x 14" rectangle for handle

From lining fabric, cut:
(2) front/back panels

(2) 2½" x 31½" rectangles for gusset

(1) 5¼" x 6½" rectangle for hinge

(1) 8" x 14" rectangle for handle

From pocket fabric, cut:
(2) 7" x 12" rectangles for zipper interior pocket

(2) 3" x 12" rectangles for zipper interior pocket

(1) 8" x 19" rectangle for gathered interior pocket

From canvas/interfacing, cut:
(2) front/back panels

(2) 2½" x 31½" rectangles for gusset

(1) 5¼" x 6½" rectangle for hinge

From batting, cut:
(2) front/back panels ½" smaller than pattern piece (following stitch line)

(2) 1½" x 30½" rectangles for gusset

(1) 4¼" x 5½" rectangle for hinge

From double-sided fusible, cut:
(2) front/back panels ½" smaller than pattern piece (following stitch line)

SEAM ALLOWANCE

½" unless otherwise noted

FINISHED SIZE

5" tall x 11¼" wide x 8½" deep

TIP: It will be helpful to mark and label your pieces for this project.

instructions

Make piping if desired (see opposite page).

Transfer all markings from pattern pieces.

QUILT FRONT/BACK PANELS AND HINGE

1. For front panel, layer canvas/interfacing, batting (centered within the panel), then exterior fabric right side up. Pin and baste along perimeter. Quilt as desired.

2. Repeat for back panel pieces and the hinge pieces using consistent/complementary quilting.

MAKE AND ATTACH HANDLE

1. Press exterior handle piece on the long edges ½" to the wrong side. Set aside.

2. Press the lining handle in half lengthwise. Open up and press raw edges to center crease. Fold in half lengthwise again, enclosing the raw edges and press. Topstitch along both long sides of lining handle. (A)

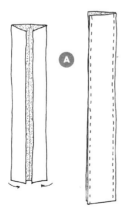

3. Pin exterior handle (wrong side down) centered on top of lining handle. Topstitch along both long edges of exterior handle, adding additional rows of topstitching in between, if desired.

4. Using a water-soluble pen, mark the center of each short side of the quilted front panel. On the raw edge or short side of each handle end, mark center. Mark a line 3" from each raw edge parallel to the side raw edges. Align center markings of handle and front panel on both sides. Baste in place along raw edges using ¼" seam allowance.

5. Pin handle down on the front panel extending a bit past the drawn line from Step 4. Topstitch along previous topstitching on handle edge through all layers, pivoting and continuing across marked line from Step 4, pivoting again and topstitching along remaining edge of the handle piece. (B)

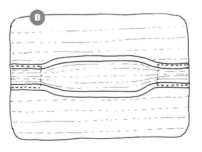

6. Repeat for remaining side of the handle. Set aside.

ASSEMBLE GATHERED INTERIOR POCKETS

1. To create the casing, press one 19" edge of the gathered interior pocket ¼" to the wrong side and press. Fold over again by ½" and press again. Edge stitch along the inner folded edge to secure the hem in place.

2. Feed elastic through the casing using a safety pin at one end of the elastic and pulling through the casing.

3. Once the elastic is pulled through, attach one side by sewing in place ⅛" from the edge of pocket. Pull elastic to opposite side and gather fabric along until the top of the pocket piece measures 12". Sew elastic in place ⅛" from the edge of the pocket piece and trim away excess elastic.

4. Sew two rows of gathering stitches across the bottom of the pocket at ⅛" and ⅜". Pull thread tails to gather until the bottom of the pocket piece measures 12".

5. Fuse double-sided stabilizer centered onto WS of lining front panel. Use parchment paper between the stabilizer and your ironing board to avoid accidental fusing. Place assembled pocket onto lining front panel with both right sides facing up and aligning the bottom and side raw edges. Baste the sides in place using ¼" seam allowance (C). Round corners of gathered pocket on bottom edge.

6. To create a divided pocket, mark a vertical line 4¼" from each side. Sew through all layers, stopping at the top of the pocket edge and backstitching to reinforce the stitching (C). Set aside.

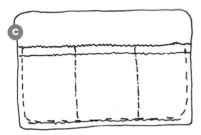

CREATE ZIPPERED POCKET

1. Place a 3" x 12" zippered pocket piece right side up and align a 10" zipper to raw edges (teeth side down) with the zipper pull at left. Place second 3" x 12" zippered pocket piece on top, right side down. Pin in place and, using your zipper foot, sew along raw edge. (D)

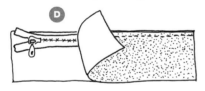

2. Position fabrics WST. Press. Topstitch along zipper.

> **TIP:** *The length and width of zipper tape varies. To account for this, the zippered pocket is designed to be taller than the finished size and trimmed after assembly. The instructions are based on using zippers that have a 1" tall x 11½" long tape. If yours is shorter, please add zipper end tabs (see page 103).*

HANDMADE PIPING

This project really pops with the help of beautifully coordinated handmade piping. It adds that special touch that store-bought piping just can't replicate. This is a perfect opportunity to use your favorite fabric and make the whole project come to life.

Piping might seem intimidating at first. Once you get a basic feel for making and using piping, you'll be adding it to all your projects!

Any dimensional project with rounded corners requires bias tape piping, so you will need a cutting mat or ruler with a 45-degree-angle marking. You'll also need ⅛" cotton cording (sometimes called cotton filler cord) and ¼" wide fusible tape.

1. Start off by cutting 1½" wide strips of your chosen piping fabric on the bias. The width of the strips is determined by the cording size and what seam allowance you'll be sewing with. For this example the piping is made to be used in a ½" seam.

2. Sew bias cut fabric strips together to join. To do this, place strip ends perpendicular to each other RST. Mark a line that runs diagonally from the upper left corner to lower right where the strips intersect. Pin. Sew along the marked line. Trim seam allowance to ¼" (A). Press seam open.

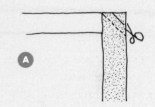

3. Place cording on center of wrong side of the fabric. Finger press fusible tape on upper one-third of fabric. Peel off paper backing. Wrap fabric over cording, bringing wrong sides of fabric together, fusing in place with an iron. (B)

That's it! You just made your own beautiful piping.

3. Repeat Step 1 using the two 7" x 12" zipper pocket pieces and working on the opposite side of zipper tape. For this step, the layers from the bottom to top will be:

1. Pocket right side up
2. Finished unit from Step 1, zipper teeth down
3. Remaining pocket right side down (E)

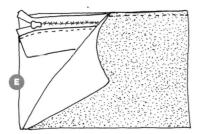

4. Fuse double-sided stabilizer centered onto wrong side of lining front panel. Use a piece of parchment paper to avoid fusing the stabilizer to your ironing board. Lay assembled zippered pocket (right sides up) on top of lining front panel and baste along all edges. Baste with front panel face up to follow curve more easily. Trim zippered pocket to match curve of back panel (F) and set aside.

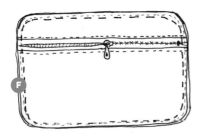

FUSE INTERIOR TO EXTERIOR

1. Place assembled zippered pocket WST with case top. The interfacing will be sandwiched between the layers. Fuse in place.

2. Repeat for assembled gathered pocket placing WST with case bottom.

ASSEMBLE GUSSET

1. Layer canvas gusset right side up, lining gusset and zipper (teeth side up). Baste into place if desired. Place exterior gusset on top of zipper, right side down. Using your zipper foot and a ¼" seam allowance, sew along zipper edge. (G)

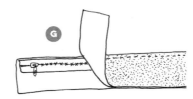

2. Position fabrics wrong sides together and press fabrics away from zipper. Sandwich batting in between the exterior and canvas and topstitch along the zipper edge (H). Baste remaining open edges together. Quilt the gusset by sewing straight horizontal lines about ⅜" apart, or as desired.

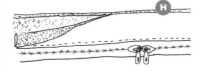

3. Repeat Steps 1–2 for the remaining pieces and the other side of zipper. (I)

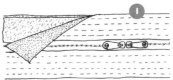

ADD HINGE

1. Aligning at one short raw edge, layer lining hinge right side up, quilted gusset exterior side up, and quilted hinge piece exterior side down. The gusset is now sandwiched between the hinge pieces with all corresponding fabrics RST. Sew along the short end (J). Press hinge away from gusset. Trim hinge height to match height of completed zipper gusset piece. Topstitch along exterior hinge through all layers.

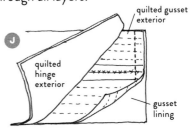

quilted gusset exterior

quilted hinge exterior

gusset lining

2. At the opposite short edge of gusset, align the quilted hinge piece and gusset with exterior fabrics RST. Do not include lining hinge in this step. Sew along the short end. Press seams toward hinge.

3. Press short edge of lining hinge ½" to the wrong side. Position lining hinge on top of quilted hinge, wrong sides together. Lining hinge should cover raw edges. Press. Pin in place. From gusset exterior, topstitch through all layers, catching lining hinge piece in stitching. You will now have a loop with concealed seams. (K)

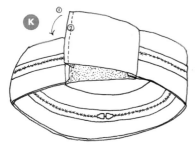

ATTACH PIPING TO EXTERIOR TOP/ BOTTOM PIECES

1. Align raw edge of piping to raw edge of exterior back panel. Beginning at center back of panel, baste in place starting 2" from raw edge of piping, continuing around panel. Clip into piping seam allowance as you reach each corner to help ease the fabric. Stop 2" from where you began.

2. Open up piping, trim cording so that ends meet, and fold one tail of piping fabric to wrong side by ½". Slip other end of piping fabric in between the piping fabric you just folded (L). Baste remaining piping in place.

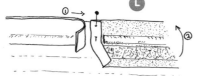

3. Repeat Steps 1-2 to attach piping to Front Panel. (M)

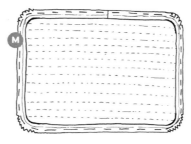

> **TIP:** *Getting the piping just right can be tricky. Using a zipper foot or piping foot, get as close to the piping as you feel comfortable. Once the seam is sewn, you can go back and stitch closer to the piping if necessary. Check your work by turning work right side out.*

ASSEMBLE CASE

1. Mark center of front/back on all four edges. Mark center on hinge piece (fold gusset/hinge loop in half to locate the center front of the unit and center of hinge) and mark with a water-soluble pen. Align center marking of front panel (bottom edge of interior zip pocket on reverse side) to hinge center. Pin in place with exteriors RST and repeat with opposite center points and short edge center points. Pin or clip to secure the gusset in place around the entire perimeter.

2. Clip ¼" into gusset piece around each rounded corner to help ease the fabric. With a piping foot (optional) sew around entire perimeter. (N)

3. Open zipper all the way to the hinge.

4. Repeat Steps 1–2 to attach gusset to the bottom panel.

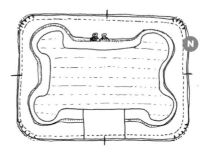

FINISH EDGES

1. With case wrong side out, align long edge of twill tape with raw edge of seam.

2. Sandwich tape around raw edges and pin in place. Sew ¼" from edge of twill tape through all layers.

3. At rounded corners stretch twill tape around edge and pin in place, slowly adjusting tape as necessary.

4. Sew around all of raw edge overlapping twill tape when you reach the beginning by turning under ½" and backstitching.

> **TIP:** *This doesn't have to be perfect, since it'll be mostly tucked in on the inside of the case. Choose a thread color to match the twill tape. The tape is just a way to enclose the raw edge, so do your best. The more you stretch the tape around the rounded corners, the less wavy the twill tape will be when finished.*

5. Repeat for raw edge of the other panel. Stock it up with your favorite travel-sized bottles and make-up and it's ready to pack.

DOUBLE ZIP WALLET

You'll love this multi-function wallet, both for its looks and for how much it holds and organizes. With two zippered openings and an inside array of pockets and card holders, it can be a stand-alone clutch or a wallet you tuck in your favorite tote. It also makes a great gift and uses a fun construction method!

style tips

▸ Using canvas or denim for the lining of this many-pocketed wallet really makes it sturdy and durable.

▸ Try quilting the exterior pieces. Using scraps pieced together would be a fun choice!

MATERIALS

Fat Quarter quilting cotton for the main panel exterior

⅓ yard 7 oz. weight canvas or denim for main panel lining

Fat Quarter quilting cotton for pockets

2" x 8¾" strip quilting cotton for the pocket binding

½ yard 20" wide fusible woven interfacing (Pellon SF101)

fusible fleece scraps

(2) 7" non-separating zippers

14mm light strength magnetic snap

zipper foot sewing machine attachment

water-soluble pen

CUTTING

See pullout for pattern pieces. Trace and cut the required pieces.

All measurements are height x width.

From exterior fabric, cut:
(2) 9" x 8¾" rectangles for the main panels

(2) 3½" squares for the tab

From canvas lining fabric, cut:
(2) 9" x 8¾" rectangles for the main panels

From pocket fabric, cut:
(1) 13½" x 8¾" rectangle for the pocket

From woven interfacing, cut:
(2) 9" x 8¾" rectangles for the main panels

(2) 3½" squares for the tabs

SEAM ALLOWANCE

½" unless otherwise noted

FINISHED SIZE

7½" x 4½" when closed, 8½" tall when open

instructions

FUSE INTERFACING

Fuse interfacing to tab and exterior main panels. Set aside.

MAKE CARD SLOTS AND INNER POCKET

1. Take the 13½" x 8¾" pocket fabric rectangle and press ½" to wrong side on one short edge. With a water-soluble pen, mark lines 2½", 4", 6", and 7½" inches down from the fold.

2. The drawn lines represent where to fold the fabric for the card slots. Fold and press along each horizontal drawn line (A). Edge stitch along both folded card slot edges.

3. To enclose the bottom raw edge with binding, press binding strip in half lengthwise, WST. Open up, then press long raw edges to center fold line. Fold in half and press again, enclosing the raw edges. Slip the binding over the bottom raw edge of the card slot piece (A). Topstitch in place on inner folded edge, being sure to catch the binding on the back side as well.

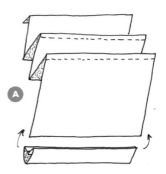

ATTACH INNER CARD SLOTS/POCKET TO EXTERIOR

1. Place assembled card slots (with top folded edge) on one exterior main panel, both right sides facing up and with card slot folded edge ½" from top short edge of main panel. Be sure the card slots are folded upward in an accordion style. Pin in place. Baste along both raw side edges through all layers using ¼" seam allowance. Topstitch along folded top edge of pocket through all layers.

2. With a water-soluble pen mark a vertical line dividing card slots in half and then a horizontal line 4" below the top edge of the exterior. (B)

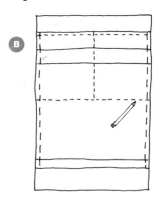

3. Sew only the vertical line, backstitching at top of card slots and where vertical line intersects the horizontal line. Do not sew on the horizontal line. This will be done later.

DIY ZIPPER LENGTH

Don't have a 7" zipper on hand? It's easy to change the length of a plastic coil zipper. Start with a zipper longer than what you need, in this case longer than 7". Measure 7" from the pull (in closed position) and make a mark on the zipper tape. With coordinating thread zigzag stitch in place across the mark several times. Trim zipper ½" past the mark.

With a metal zipper it's a little trickier, but it can be done! Mark the length you need, measuring from the bottom end stop (which is opposite of what you would do with a plastic coil zipper). Use side snippers or needle nose pliers and gently pull off the top stop and any teeth up until the mark. Reinstall the top end stop (or new end stops can be purchased at most fabric stores). Trim the zipper tape ½" past the mark you made. Done! That wasn't too hard, was it?

MAKE TAB

1. On wrong side of one tab piece, mark sewing line and the magnetic snap placement using traced template from the pattern pullout as a guide.

2. Insert magnetic snap at the mark using the washer to mark prong placement. Cut prong slits with sharp scissors. Push pronged snap through from right side of fabric. Cut prong slits and slip scrap of fusible fleece over prongs. Slip washer over prongs. Bend prongs out to sides (C). Place another scrap of woven fusible over the top and fuse it all in place.

3. Place tab pieces right sides together. Sew along marked sewing line leaving the straight edge unsewn. Notch curves, and trim remaining fabric to a ¼" seam allowance. Turn right side out. Press. Topstitch again, leaving the top unsewn. (D)

TIP: *If sewing near the snap with an all-purpose presser foot is difficult, try using your zipper foot.*

4. With raw edge of tab aligned with raw edge of exterior main panel, center tab on the side opposite the card slot, and with the snap facing down. Baste in place. (E)

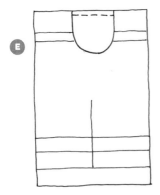

ASSEMBLE

1. Fold back both zipper tape ends at a 45-degree angle and secure in place with a few stitches (F). Repeat for the opposite zipper ends and again for the second zipper. Set one zipper aside.

2. Place exterior main panel right side up with tab edge at top. Place and center zipper (teeth side down) with pull at left and raw edges aligned. On top, place canvas lining main panel on the short edge right side down. Pin in place, then using your zipper foot attachment, sew along zipper using ¼" seam allowance.

3. Position fabrics wrong sides together. Press. Topstitch along zipper lifting the tab out of the way (G). This will be referred to as Unit A.

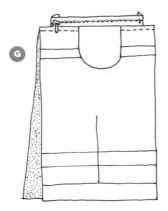

4. Repeat with remaining zipper and second exterior/canvas lining main panels. Place and center zipper pull (teeth side down) at left on top of right side of exterior. Place canvas lining panel on top, right sides together. Sew through all layers using ¼" seam allowance. Position fabrics WST. Press. Topstitch along zipper (H). This will be referred to as Unit B. You will now have two separate units with zippers installed.

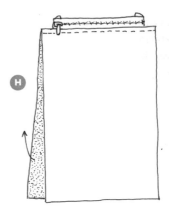

5. Separate fabrics of Unit B so that lining is right side up with raw edge at top of work surface. Center zipper from Unit A along top raw edge of Unit B. Raw edges will be aligned and tab will be face up at top of unit. Bring remaining (exterior) half of Unit B up and place on top of Unit A, RST. Unit A will need to bunch up slightly for raw edges to meet at top. Sew using a ¼" seam allowance, backstitching at each end. Turn project right sides out. Press. Topstitch along zipper. (I)

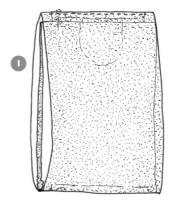

6. With assembled Unit B exterior panel at top and card slot Unit A exterior at bottom, bring exterior card slot piece and lining piece up in opposite directions and sandwich around zipper of Unit B. You will slightly bunch up Unit B fabrics just as you did in Step 5 in order for raw edges to match. (J)

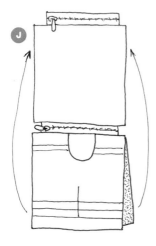

7. Sew through all layers using ¼" seam allowance, backstitching at each end. (K)

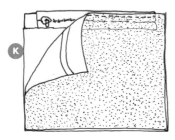

8. Turn the assembled wallet exterior side out. Lining will be WST with corresponding exterior panels. Topstitch along zipper.

TIP: *Topstitching along the zipper is going to be a bit awkward. The wallet is essentially a tube at this point in construction. Open zipper and smooth fabrics out away from zipper as best you can while topstitching and go slow.*

INSTALL OTHER HALF OF MAGNETIC SNAP

1. Position zippers at opposite (outer) edges. Fold the wallet in half with card slots on interior. Use the horizontal marking on the card slot piece as a guide.

NOTE: *The zippers will be offset by ½".*

2. Fold tab over front zipper. With a water-soluble pen, mark where center of magnetic snap on tab hits the exterior of the wallet. (L)

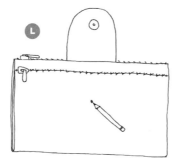

3. Repeat Step 2 of *Make Tab* (see page 99) to install magnetic snap through exterior, reaching in through sides to get to back side of exterior to install snap. Snap will only be installed through exterior layer of the wallet.

FINISH

1. Turn wallet wrong side out so the exterior pieces and lining pieces are RST, forming a tube (reach between one exterior lining layer and turn tube wrong side out). Be sure to push zipper teeth toward lining pieces and open the zippers halfway. Sew along both raw edges of tube. On one side of the tube, leave a 4" opening on the lining for turning. (M)

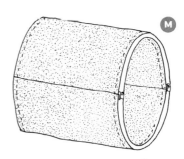

2. Trim the lining seam allowance to ¼". Turn right side out through opening in lining. Sew opening shut by machine or hand, tucking in raw edges and using a ⅛" seam allowance.

3. Turn wallet so that the lining pieces are RST. Push out corners.

4. Press well along sides then fold in half using the line you marked in step 2 of making the card slots. Zippers will be offset by ½".

5. Through all layers, sew along horizontal marked line on card slot piece to divide inner pocket into two. Fun to make and fun to give!

GINGHAM TOTE

This hardworking tote will be your go-to bag to bring wherever life takes you! I give you two great pocket options — one is a little bit easier and the other gives you more of a challenge. Either way, you'll be proud to carry this around town. The adjustable shoulder strap makes it easy to carry, and the short handles are a convenient alternative.

style tips

▸ Mix and match: cut each front pocket piece out of a different favorite fabric!

▸ Try a quilt-as-you-go patchwork for the body. Use chambray for the pocket to make the patchwork shine.

MATERIALS

¾ yard home dec, canvas, or denim for exterior

½ yard quilting cotton for lining

¾ yard quilting cotton for pocket and strap

½ yard quilting cotton for pocket lining

3 yards 20" wide fusible woven interfacing (Pellon SF101)

fusible fleece scraps

(2) 7" non-separating zippers, or (1) 7" non-separating zipper for rounded pocket

1½" adjustable strap slider and (2) 1½" metal rectangles

18mm magnetic snap

(10) 8mm rivets (optional)

(2) ¾" x 15" leather straps (optional)

zipper foot sewing machine attachment

tracing paper

water-soluble pen

CUTTING

TIP: *It will be helpful to mark and label your pieces for this project.*

All measurements are height x width.

From exterior, cut:
(2) 16½" x 15½" rectangles for main panel

(2) 4" x 15½" rectangles for lining reinforcement strips

From lining, cut:
(2) 13½" x 15½" rectangles for lining panel

From pocket fabric, cut:
(2) 6" x WOF strips for cross-body strap
Subcut:
(2) 6" x 4" strap holders

▸ For double zip pocket version, cut:
(2) 2¾" x 9" rectangles for top zipper pocket

(2) 3½" x 9" rectangles for middle zipper pocket

(2) 7½" x 9" rectangles for bottom zipper pocket

(1) 13¾" by 9" rectangle for large pocket lining

(8) 1" x 1½" rectangles for zipper end tabs

▸ For rounded pocket version, cut:
See pullout for pattern piece. Trace and cut the required piece.

(2) 2¾" x 9" rectangles for top pocket

(2) bottom pockets tracing pattern pullout

(1) rounded pocket lining tracing pattern pullout

(4) 1" x 1½" rectangles for zipper end tabs

From pocket lining, cut:
(2) 8" x 15½" rectangles for interior slip pocket

(1) 13¾" x 9" rectangle for zippered pocket lining, or (1) rounded zippered pocket lining tracing pattern pullout

(2) 3" x 15½" strips for short handles (if not using leather straps)

From woven interfacing, cut:
(2) 16½" x 15½" rectangles for main panel

(2) 13½" x 15½" rectangles for lining panel

(2) 4" x 15½" strips for lining reinforcement strips

(3) 6" x 20" strips for cross-body strap

(2) 3" x 15½" strips for short handles (if not using leather straps)

(1) 8" x 15½" rectangle for interior slip pocket

SEAM ALLOWANCE

½" unless otherwise noted

FINISHED SIZE

14" tall x 14" wide x 3" deep

instructions

FUSE INTERFACING AND PREPARE PIECES

1. Fuse interfacing to the wrong side of all corresponding pieces (except the cross-body strap).

2. With a water-soluble pen, mark a 1½" square in both bottom corners of each short side of the main panel. Cut out the square in each corner. Repeat for lining panels.

PREPARE STRAPS

1. Sew cross-body strap pieces short ends RST and trim to 60" in length. Fuse interfacing end to end on the wrong side. Press short ends of strap in by ¼" to the wrong side.

2. Press in half lengthwise, WST. Open and press long raw edges to fold line. Press. Fold in half again enclosing the raw edges and press. Topstitch along both long edges. Add additional rows of topstitching as desired (A). Set aside.

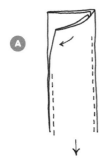

3. Press short ends in by ¼" to wrong side and repeat Step 2 for the two short handle pieces if not using leather for the strap holders.

4. Repeat Step 2 for strap holders.

5. Loop strap holder through rectangular hardware piece. Align raw edges and baste in place (B). Repeat for remaining strap holder. Set aside.

PREPARE ZIPPERS

1. Trim zipper tape to ½" past the zipper stop at both ends.

2. Lay zipper end tab right side up. Place zipper (teeth side up) aligning to short edge of zipper end tab. Place remaining zipper end tab right side down on top. Pin through all layers. Using your zipper foot attachment, sew as close to the zipper end stop as you feel comfortable. Position end tabs WST. Press away from zipper. Topstitch along edge of tab (C). Repeat for remaining zipper end tabs and remaining zipper if making the double zip pocket.

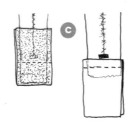

3. If necessary trim assembled zippers to overall length of 9". (D)

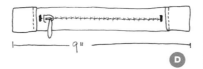

MAKE FRONT POCKET
Double zip pocket version

1. Place one middle zipper pocket panel right side up and align zipper tape of one zipper (teeth side down) to top raw edge. Repeat for the second zipper but aligning to bottom raw edge. Both zippers will have the pull to the left. Baste in place along zipper tapes using ⅛" seam.

2. Place remaining middle zipper pocket panel right side down on top of zippers. Using your zipper foot attachment, sew along top edge and bottom edge using a ¼" seam allowance and backstitching at both ends. (E)

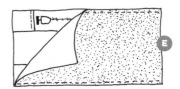

3. Turn this tube right side out. Press. Topstitch along both of the long seams. (F)

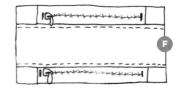

4. Place one top zipper pocket panel right side up and lay assembled middle zipper unit from Step 3 on top (zipper's teeth side down) with zipper pulls at right, aligning top raw edges. Lay remaining top zipper pocket panel right side down on top, aligning to top raw edge. Pin in place. With your zipper foot, sew using a ¼" seam allowance. Position top zipper pocket panels WST. Press away from zipper unit. Topstitch along seam next to the zipper. (G)

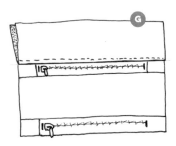

5. Place bottom zipper pocket panel right side up and lay assembled zippered pocket on top with zipper's teeth side up and pulls at right. Align zipper tape to top long raw edge of bottom zipper pocket panel. Lay remaining bottom zipper pocket panel right side down on top, aligning long edge to zipper tape. Pin in place. With your zipper foot, sew using a ¼" seam allowance. (H)

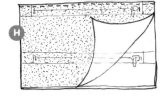

6. Position bottom zipper pocket fabrics WST. Press away from zipper and topstitch along seam next to the zipper. (I)

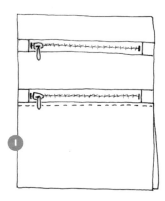

7. Place zippered pocket lining right side up, lay assembled zippered pocket (lining side down) on top. Trim zippered pocket lining to match assembled zippered pocket, if necessary. Baste in place along both side edges. (J)

8. Place large pocket lining right side down on top of assembled zippered pocket from Step 5, trim large pocket lining to match if necessary. With a ⅜" seam allowance, sew along sides and top, leaving bottom edge unsewn. Clip top corners. Turn right side out. Push out corners. Press.

9. Topstitch along top edge of assembled pocket. Topstitch over existing topstitching above bottom zipper (K). This separates the zippered pockets into two.

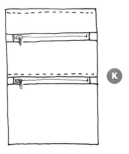

10. Baste bottom of pocket.

ROUNDED POCKET ALTERNATE

1. Place one alternate top pocket panel right side up and align zipper tape (teeth side up) to top raw edge, with zipper pull on the left. Baste in place along zipper tape. Place remaining alternate top pocket panel right side down on top of zipper. Using your zipper foot, sew along zipper edges using a ¼" seam allowance. (L)

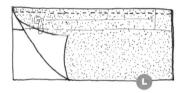

2. Position alternate top pocket pieces wrong sides together. Press. Topstitch along seam next to the zipper. (M)

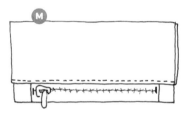

3. Place one alternate bottom pocket panel right side up with straight edge at the top. Place assembled zippered pocket on top with zipper (teeth side down) and pull at left. Align zipper tape to top 9" edge of alternate bottom pocket panel. Lay remaining alternate bottom pocket panel right side down on top, aligning to zipper tape. Pin in place. With your zipper foot, sew using a ¼" seam allowance. (N)

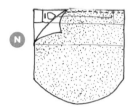

4. Position alternate bottom pocket panels wrong sides together. Press. Topstitch along seam next to the zipper. (O)

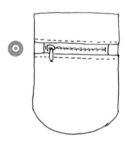

5. Place alternate rounded zippered pocket lining right side up. Place assembled zippered pocket (lining side down) on top. Trim pocket lining to match assembled zipper pocket, if necessary. Baste in place along all edges using a scant seam allowance

6. Place alternate rounded pocket lining right side down on top of assembled zippered pocket, trim rounded pocket lining if necessary and pin in place. With a ⅜" seam allowance, sew around entire perimeter, leaving a 4" opening along top pocket edge. Clip corners and notch at the curve (P). Turn right side out. Push out corners. Press. Tuck in raw edges at pocket top. Press. Topstitch along top edge of assembled pocket, catching the opening in stitches.

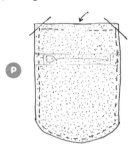

ASSEMBLE MAIN

1. Finger press main exterior panel in half to find center and mark on both top and bottom edges. Finger press assembled zippered pocket in half and mark center on top and bottom edges. Place assembled zippered pocket, lining side down on main exterior panel. Align pocket to bottom raw edge and center by aligning markings. For the alternate rounded pocket, place pocket 3¼" below the top raw edge (R, page 106). Pin in place.

2. Mark a horizontal line on assembled zippered pocket 2" from bottom raw edge (skip this step for the alternate rounded pocket version).

3. Attach assembled pocket by edge stitching along one pocket's side starting at the top corner, reinforcing with triangle shape, and sewing to the bottom edge. Repeat for the other edge. Sew across the marked line from previous step through all layers. (Q)

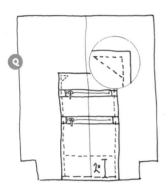

4. For the alternate rounded pocket, edge stitch along sides and curved pocket edges, reinforcing the top corners by starting and ending with triangle shape in each corner. Top edge will remain unsewn. To further reinforce the top pocket edge, install rivets at each top pocket corner. See page 75 for instructions on how to install rivets. (R)

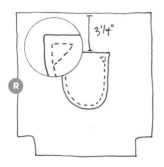

5. Place main exterior panels RST and sew along side and bottom seams (S). Press seams open.

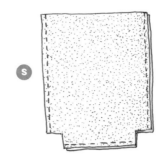

6. Box corners by reaching into bag and pinching one corner together, aligning bottom seam to corresponding side seam. Pin. Sew (T). Repeat for second corner. Turn right side out.

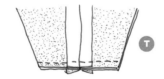

7. Baste strap holders centered on each side seam with raw edges of strap aligned with raw edges of bag top, right sides together. (U)

ASSEMBLE LINING

1. Place reinforcement strip and lining panel RST along the short edge of lining panel and sew. Press seam allowance toward reinforcement strip. Topstitch along seam on reinforcement strip. Repeat for remaining strip and lining pieces.

2. Place slip pocket panels RST. Sew along only the top and bottom (longer) edges. Turn right side out. Press. Topstitch along top edge.

3. Place assembled slip pocket panel 4½" below the top raw edge of reinforcement strip. Pin and baste along both sides, using ⅛" seam allowance. Sew along bottom edge of slip pocket. Fold lining in half and finger press to find center. Mark a line vertically through the slip pocket at the center. Sew on the marked line, being sure to backstitch at the top and bottom. You now have a divided interior slip pocket. (V)

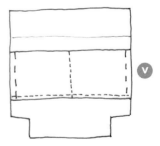

4. Insert magnetic snap (see page 99) to reinforcement strip, centered, 2" down from top raw edge. Repeat for remaining half of snap and remaining reinforcement strip.

5. Place assembled lining panels RST. Sew along sides and bottom, leaving a 5" opening for turning (W). Box corners as in Step 5 of *Assemble Main* (see page 105).

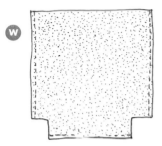

FINAL ASSEMBLY

1. Place exterior into assembled lining, with the tote back RST with interior slip pockets. Align the side seams and pin. Sew along top opening of tote. Turn right side out through opening in lining. (X)

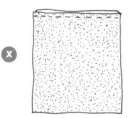

2. Sew lining opening closed by tucking in raw edges and sewing or hand stitching shut.

3. Push lining into exterior. Press at bag opening, rolling lining slightly lower than exterior. Topstitch along tote opening.

4. Topstitch along top opening using a longer stitch length (such as 3.0mm).

5. Take one end of cross-body strap and loop over middle bar of strap slider hardware piece. Fold it over so it bends back on itself, overlapping by 2". Sew in place through all layers. (Y)

6. Take remaining strap end, thread through one strap holder's rectangular hardware. (Z)

7. Loop strap up and over the center bar of the slider hardware piece and back down the other side. Take care to keep the strap from twisting during this process. Thread the end through the remaining strap holder's hardware, inserting from the outside of the hardware to match the look on the other side of the bag.

8. Fold strap back onto itself, overlapping by 2". Sew in place through all strap layers. (AA)

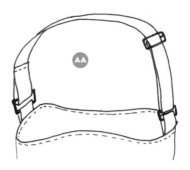

9. Locate placement of short handles by marking the center on the exterior top edge. Then mark 2½" from each side of the center. Align inside edge of handle to those markings with the bottom handle edge 1¾" down from finished top edge of bag. Sew through all layers, making a rectangle on each handle end and adding an X for added strength. (Or you can use optional leather straps and two rivets to reinforce each handle end) (AB). Ready to take out and about!

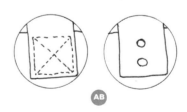

RAINBOW CLUTCH

You'll love making this sweet little clutch for yourself or your friends. It's great for stashing a few essentials and going out on the town. A beautiful patchwork front pocket detail is a great place to feature your favorite small scraps, or make it one piece and highlight that one print you love! A zip top and zippered back pocket help keep all your belongings secure.

style tips

▶ The front pocket provides an opportunity to use your favorite fabrics. Or, for a more streamlined look, you could opt not to piece the pocket. Metal zippers give this clutch a professional look. If you're uneasy about using metal zippers, though, plastic coil zippers work just as well!

MATERIALS

¼ yard quilting cotton for the exterior

⅓ yard quilting cotton for the lining

(5) 5" x 6" (or larger) scraps of quilting cotton for exterior patchwork pocket

½ yard 20"-wide fusible woven interfacing (Pellon SF101)

Scraps of fusible fleece

8" non-separating zipper

7" non-separating zipper

14mm lightweight magnetic snap

fabric glue stick

zipper foot sewing machine attachment

tracing paper

water-soluble pen

CUTTING

See pullout for pattern pieces. Trace patterns, photocopy the paper piecing pattern and cut the required pieces.

All measurements are height x width.

From exterior, cut:
(2) Main panels

(2) 3¾" x 4½" rectangles for the flap pieces

(2) 1½" x 1¾" rectangles for the zipper end tabs

From lining, cut:
(2) Main panels

(1) Front Pocket

(1) 9" x 10" rectangle for the back zipper pocket lining

From interfacing, cut:
(2) Main panels

(1) Front Pocket

(2) 3¾" x 4½" rectangles for the flap

SEAM ALLOWANCE

½" unless otherwise noted

FINISHED SIZE

9" wide x 5" tall x 1½" deep

instructions

Transfer all markings from pattern pieces.

FUSE INTERFACING

Fuse the interfacing to the wrong side of the exterior main panels and one tab piece. Set aside.

MAKE FLAP

1. On wrong side of one tab, use a water-soluble pen to mark sewing line ½" from raw edges using the pattern piece as guide (see pattern Pullout). Transfer magnetic snap placement marking from pattern piece, use washer from the magnetic snap to mark prong placement. Install magnetic snap (see page 99). Place flap pieces right sides together. (A)

2. Sew along marked sewing line, leaving top edge unsewn. Trim excess fabric from around flap ¼" from the sewn line. Notch curves and turn right side out. Press.

3. Topstitch along sides and curves leaving the top unsewn.

4. With one main exterior panel right side up, align top edge of flap with raw edge of exterior panel. Center flap, with the snap facing main exterior, and baste in place along the top. Set aside.

MAKE PATCHWORK POCKET

1. Begin paper piecing the patchwork pocket (see paper piecing tip page 110) by placing a scrap of quilting cotton WST on the non-printed side of the paper, covering marked center of section 3. Be sure this center strip covers all areas and extends ¼" past each side of the center strip markings. (B)

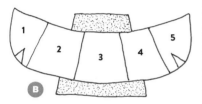

2. Use a fabric glue stick or a fine pin to temporarily hold in place.

3. Crease right edge of section 3 paper and fold paper back on itself along the line between sections 3 and 4. Trim fabric ¼" away from folded paper edge (C). Working toward section 5, lay next scrap of quilting cotton RST with the fabric on section 3, aligning the cut edges.

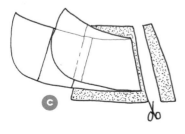

4. Test by placing a pin in the stitching line and flip the second strip over to be sure it covers all areas ¼" beyond section 4. Unfold paper and using a shorter stitch length, with paper side up, sew through all layers following the marked line. (D)

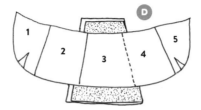

5. Press second strip toward section 5.

6. Repeat Steps 3–5 for the remaining scraps of patchwork pieces. After all patchwork is complete, give the entire unit a final press and remove the paper, tearing carefully along the stitch lines.

7. Transfer patchwork seam lines from front pocket pattern piece to non-fusible side of interfacing.

8. Fuse interfacing to wrong side of pieced patchwork pocket, aligning patchwork seams to markings. Cut front pocket from pieced patchwork, following perimeter of the interfacing.

9. Transfer and mark darts on wrong side of patchwork pocket (E). Sew darts by aligning dart legs so the right sides are touching. Sew along dart leg. Unlike in garment construction, backstitching at both ends of the dart will keep everything secure. Press darts toward outer edges.

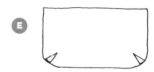

10. Repeat Step 9 for the pocket lining, exterior main and lining panels. Press darts inward on the lining and outward on the main panels.

11. Place completed patchwork pocket right sides together with front pocket lining. With a ¼" seam allowance sew along top edge. Notch curve. Position so wrong sides are together. Press.

12. Topstitch along pocket top edge.

13. Place pocket on main panel and with flap. Mark snap placement on pocket (¼" higher than where the snap actually aligns). (F)

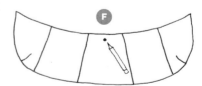

14. Attach the remaining half of the magnetic snap to the pocket exterior following Step 1 from the *Make Flap* (see page 108) construction. Replace pocket on main panel and baste along sides and bottom through all layers (G). Set aside.

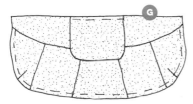

INSERT BACK ZIPPERED POCKET

1. On wrong side of pocket lining, mark a 7¼" wide x ½" tall rectangle centered 1¼" down from the 10" edge of the zipper pocket lining.

2. Center 10" edge of pocket lining to top raw edge of back exterior main panel of clutch RST. Pin and stitch on marked rectangle through all of the layers. (H)

3. With sharp scissors, cut through all layers along center of rectangle angling out to corners when you reach each end. Clip to corner but not through the stitching. (H)

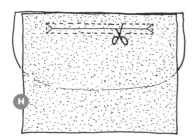

PAPER PIECING

Paper piecing can seem backward at times. If this is a new technique for you, give it a few tries with some scrap fabric first. It helps to have a special sewing machine needle saved specifically for paper piecing since the needle can dull while sewing through paper. Just set it aside and mark for future paper piecing use. A short stitch length (2.0mm) helps with tearing away paper after all pieces are complete. There are many helpful paper piecing videos online if you're feeling stuck or frustrated.

4. Push pocket lining through the cut opening to the back side of the clutch so that fabrics are WST. This part can be somewhat tricky — just take your time and finger press the seam. Press.

5. Place a 7" zipper behind opening, ensuring that zipper pull is within the opening and pin in place or use ¼" fusible tape to temporarily hold it in place. With a zipper foot, topstitch along edge of opening around the whole rectangle to securely attach the zipper. (I)

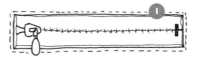

6. Working from wrong side of clutch back main panel, fold pocket lining up, right sides touching and aligning with top raw edge of pocket lining. Sew pocket lining along sides, being sure to keep main clutch panel away from seam. Sew pocket lining to main panel along top raw edge through all of the layers using a ⅛" seam allowance. (J)

SEW ZIPPER END TABS

1. Press zipper end tabs in half widthwise RST. Open up and press short ends of zipper end tabs to center crease, WST. Fold in half again, encasing raw edges in the center. Press.

2. Trim 8" zipper tape ends ½" from both zipper end stops. (K)

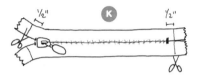

3. Slip end tab over zipper tape. Topstitch along inner fold, being sure to avoid the metal end stops.

4. Repeat Step 3 for the other zipper end tab. Once end tabs are sewn on, total length should measure no more than 9" (L). Trim off any excess tab fabric to match the width of the zipper tape.

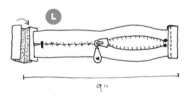

ASSEMBLE

1. Lay exterior front main panel face up. Center the zipper (teeth side down, with pull at left) along top raw edge of exterior. Center the main lining right side down on top of zipper. Pin in place. Sew using a ¼" seam allowance.

2. Position fabrics WST. Press. Topstitch along zipper, lifting front tab out of the way so you don't catch it in the topstitching. (M)

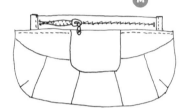

3. Lay exterior back main panel face up. Center the zipper (teeth side down, with pull at right), aligning top raw edge of exterior to zipper tape. Center the lining right side down on top of the zipper. Pin. Sew using ¼" seam allowance.

4. Position fabrics WST. Press. Topstitch along zipper.

5. Open zipper halfway. Position fabrics so that exteriors are RST and linings are RST.

TIP: *In order to get the zipper ends to come out square, it is important to push the zipper end tabs toward the lining. Be sure to pin them in place. They'll be pinched in half facing down into the lining. Don't sew through the tabs on the next step, but approx. ⅛" away from them. You won't be able to see them, but feel for the tabs through the layers.*

6. Sew along perimeter of both exterior and lining, leaving a 4" opening in lining (N). Trim lining seam allowance to ¼" and notch exterior curves. Pull right side out through opening in lining. Push out the corners and tuck the raw edges of lining into opening. Sew closed by hand or by machine using a small seam allowance.

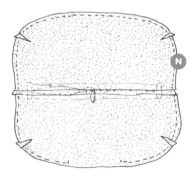

7. Push lining into clutch. Give it one final press and it's ready for a night out on the town.

PICNIC PLAID QUILT

This quilt is all about value — color value, that is. In this example, I used dark values for the large pluses, light values for the small pluses, and medium values for the background to really play with the contrast. Where you place the fabrics in your quilt can give this project a whole different look!

TIP: *You will have scrap strips left over. Why not use these to create a pieced backing?*

instructions

MAKE SMALL PLUSES

1. Sew a 3" strip of medium value fabric to each side of 3" light value fabric strip. Repeat to sew a total of (2)(7)(15)(26) strip sets. (A)

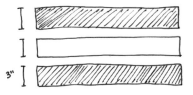

3"

Ⓐ

style tips

▸ All solids would be especially stunning in this quilt. Take time to carefully choose your fabrics.

▸ Color-building palettes online can be helpful. They allow you to use a picture to help you select colors for your quilt.

TIP: *I made this quilt using one fabric for the light value and another for the medium value pieces. To add variety, each block can be cut using fat quarters (FQs). You can use 1, 4, 9, or 16 different ones for each color value depending on the size you make.*

CUTTING

Locate and circle the cutting instructions for the quilt size you are making. Quilts are listed in this order: (pillow)(baby)(lap)(family)

From each dark value FQ or ¼ yard, cut:

(1) 5" x 20" rectangle

(2) 5" x 8" rectangles

From medium value fabric, cut:
(2)(7)(15)(26) 3" x WOF strips

Subcut into (4)(14)(30)(52) 3" x 20" strips

From light value fabric, cut:
(2)(8)(16)(26) 3" x WOF strips

Separate half of the strips. Subcut these into a total of (2)(7)(15)(26) 3" x 20" strips

Cut remaining WOF strips into a total of (4)(16)(36)(64) 3" x 8" rectangles

From binding fabric, cut:
(n/a)(4)(7)(8) 2¼" x WOF strips

SEAM ALLOWANCE
¼" unless otherwise noted

FINISHED SIZE:
see below

MATERIALS: USE QUILTING COTTON THROUGHOUT				
	PILLOW	BABY	LAP	FAMILY
Finished Size	19½" x 19½"	39" x 39"	59" x 59"	77" x 77"
Number of Blocks	1	4	9	16
Dark Value Fabric	(1) FQ or ¼ yard	(4) FQs or ¼ yard	(9) FQs or ¼ yard	(16) FQs or ¼ yard
Medium Value Fabric	¼ yard	¾ yard	1⅓ yards	2¼ yards
Light Value Fabric	¼ yard	¾ yard	1½ yards	2¼ yards
Backing	¾ yard	2½ yards	3¾ yards	4¾ yards
Binding	NA	⅓ yard	½ yard	⅔ yard
Batting (90" wide batting by the yard)	⅔ yard	1¼ yards	2 yards	2½ yards

2. Square up end of strip set and subcut strips into 3" widths to make (8)(32)(72)(128) units. (B)

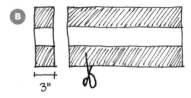

3. Sew one strip unit to each side of a 3" x 8" light value fabric rectangle. Press seam toward darker fabric. (C)

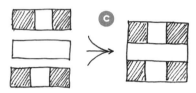

ATTACH TO DARK VALUE FABRIC UNIT

1. Sew small pluses to each side of a 5" x 8" dark value fabric unit along 8" edge. Press seam toward darker fabric. (D)

2. Repeat for remaining small pluses and 5" x 8" dark value center piece. (E)

COLOR VALUE

You've heard of the term 'value', right? In terms of color, value is the lightness or darkness of a fabric. It sounds simple enough but can be tricky to determine. For this project you'll be selecting your fabrics based on their value. This helps reinforce the design and makes the quilt really sing. A great way to confirm that you have picked the right value order is to take a black and white picture of your fabric choices together. By removing the color from the picture, you're able to see how light or dark the fabrics truly are. For instance, even though they aren't the same color, a dark maroon and a dark gray both have a dark value. A white fabric with a small-scale design appears as a light value. Same with a pale pink or light yellow—they're both light value, too. Struggling to find the medium value? Just grab your dark and light value selections and make sure your medium value choices are in between the two! Depending on your fabric choices, there can be a wide range of values used here. The success of this design is not dependent on the fabrics themselves; rather, how accurately you separate your fabrics into their different value groups.

COMPLETE THE BLOCK

1. Sew small-plus assembled units to both sides of the dark value fabric 5" x 20" piece along 20" edge (F). Press seams toward darker fabric.

PILLOW FINISHING

1. Make one block for pillow. See page 127 for making a pillow using a 20" invisible zipper. Make four blocks for a baby quilt. Make nine blocks for a lap quilt. Make 16 blocks for a family size quilt.

2. Sew (n/a)(2)(3)(4) blocks each into (n/a)(2)(3)(4) rows, then sew rows together to form quilt top. Be sure to press seams to one side, alternating directions with each row to nest all of the seams.

QUILT FINISHING

1. If making a quilt, layer backing, batting and quilt top together and baste.

2. Quilt as desired and attach binding using your favorite method. If quilt making is new to you, download the free PDF of Quilt Making Basics from the luckyspool.com website.

UP & DOWN QUILT

Love things trianglular? Want a quilt that will make a statement on your bed? This is a fun and fast quilt for its size. This quilt uses fat quarters for the main triangles, so you can have a great time mixing and matching your favorite prints or solids for a beautiful and bold quilt.

style tips

▸ Think of using a dark background fabric with bright or light fabrics for the triangles.

▸ Carefully place the colors in the large triangles to create an even more distinct pattern. Use darker value triangles for the top, middle, and point, and light value (or even background fabric) for the remaining triangles.

MATERIALS

10 fat quarters (FQs) for triangles

4½ yards quilting cotton for the background

5½ yards quilting cotton for the backing

¾ yard quilting cotton for the binding

2½ yards low-loft cotton batting

CUTTING

See pullout for pattern pieces. Trace and cut the required pieces.

From each FQ, cut:
  (2) large triangles for main triangles

From one FQ, cut:
  (2) small triangle pattern pieces

From background fabric, cut:
  (2) 8½" x 39½" top/bottom borders

  (4) 13½" x 36" side borders

  (1) 6" x 39½" center strip

  (4) 8½" x 13½" quilt corners

  (2) 6" x 8" rectangles

  (2) background small half-triangle pattern pieces

  (2) mirror image of background small half-triangle pattern pieces

  (12) large triangle pattern pieces

  (6) background large half-triangle pattern pieces

  (6) mirror image of background large half-triangle pattern pieces

From binding fabric, cut:
  (9) 2½" x WOF strips

SEAM ALLOWANCE
¼" unless otherwise noted

FINISHED SIZE
65" x 88"

instructions

PIECE LARGE PATCHWORK TRIANGLES

1. Arrange large triangles cut from your FQs into a pleasing combination in rows of five, three, and one to create a pieced triangle layout. (A)

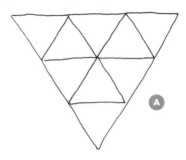

2. Referencing the Quilt Assembly diagram (see opposite page), arrange background triangles and half triangles into the three rows from Step 1.

3. Beginning with the first piece in the row, place two triangle pieces RST, aligning notches. Sew along one edge (B). Press seam open. Place another triangle on opposite side and sew. Repeat to complete each row.

4. Join the three rows together, pressing seams open. You will now have one large pieced triangle block, measuring 39½" wide. (C)

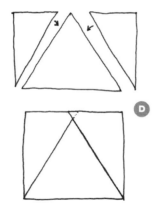

5. Repeat Steps 1-4 for the second pieced triangle block.

PIECE SMALL TRIANGLES

1. Align notches and attach a small background half-triangle to both long sides of a small triangle (D). Press seams open. Block should measure 6" square.

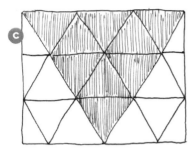

2. Repeat for remaining small triangle unit.

ASSEMBLE QUILT TOP

1. Referencing Quilt Assembly Diagram for block orientation, lay out remaining units into a total of 5 Rows.

Rows 1 and 5: For Row 1, attach an 8½" x 13½" corner piece to each side of an 8 ½" x 39½" top/bottom border. Press seams open. Repeat for Row 5.

Rows 2 and 4: For Row 2, center and attach a 13½" x 36" side border to either side of a large pieced triangle block. The border will be longer than the pieced triangle block. Press seams open. Trim border to the length of pieced triangle block. Repeat for Row 4.

Row 3: Attach a 6" x 8" background rectangle to a small pieced triangle block.

Repeat for the second small pieced triangle block. Attach to either side of the 6" x 39½" center strip. Press seams open.

2. Assemble rows together, being sure to pin and match your seams at each intersection. Press seams open.

FINISHING

1. Layer backing, batting and quilt top together and baste.

2. Quilt as desired and attach binding using your favorite method. If quilt making is new to you, download the free PDF of Quilt Making Basics from the luckyspool.com website.

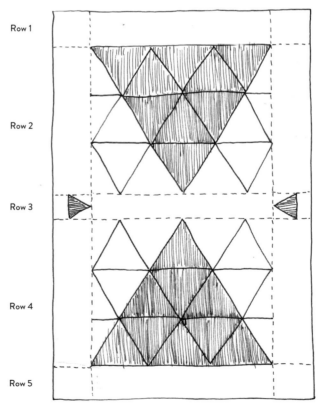

QUILT ASSEMBLY DIAGRAM

ARROW QUILT

Bring together your favorite colors and fabrics and let them shine in this simple yet bold small quilt! This is a great exercise in limiting your color palette to three main colors. Graphic shapes and easy construction make this pattern a quick and fun finish, perfect for either the wall or a stroller blanket. The arrow creates a focal point in any room, making the quilt an especially thoughtful gift for a modern nursery.

style tips

▸ Try using a cuddly flannel or soft shot cotton for the backing if you're making this as a stroller blanket. The softer the better!

▸ Experiment with your quilting! Straight lines are always a great choice, but consider taking this opportunity to use free-motion quilting and vary your designs on each segment.

MATERIALS

½ yard quilting cotton for arrows

¼ yard quilting cotton for corners

1 yard quilting cotton for the background

1⅛ yard quilting cotton for the backing

½ yard quilting cotton for the binding

crib size package OR 1 yard low-loft cotton batting

water-soluble pen

CUTTING

From arrow fabric, cut:
(4) 7¼" x 4" rectangles for the arrow legs

(1) 12" square

From corner fabric, cut:
(4) 8" squares

From background fabric, cut:
(1) 4" square for the center

(4) 5¼" x 4¼" rectangles

(4) 5¼" squares

(4) 7¼" squares

(1) 12" square

(4) 2½" x WOF strips for the borders, then subcut into (2) 27" strips and (2) 32" strips

From binding fabric, cut:
(4) 2½" x WOF strips

SEAM ALLOWANCE
¼" unless otherwise noted

FINISHED SIZE
30" square

instructions

MAKE HALF-SQUARE TRIANGLES

1. Place 12" squares RST. Mark a diagonal line from corner to corner. Repeat on opposite side to create an X. With a short stitch length (1.8mm–2.0mm), sew ¼" from either side of the drawn line. (A)

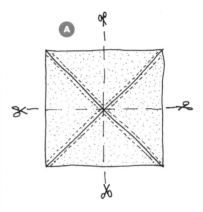

2. Using a straight edge and a rotary cutter, cut on both drawn lines and then cut in half vertically and horizontally.

3. Press all seams open. You will now have 8 half-square triangles (HSTs). Trim each HST to 5¼" and set aside.

PIECE CENTER BLOCK

1. Referencing Figure C for block orientation lay out three rows in the following order:

Rows 1 and 3: Attach a 7¼" background square to each long side of a 7¼" x 4" rectangle. Press seams open.

Row 2: Attach a 7¼" x 4" rectangle to opposite sides of a 4" square.

ADD ARROW BORDERS

1. Referencing Figure C for block orientation, lay out the arrow borders.

2. Assemble two strips of: 5¼" x 4¼" background rectangle, HST, HST, 5¼" x 4¼" background rectangle. Press seams open.

3. Attach strip units to the top and bottom of the assembled center block. Press seams open.

4. Assemble two strips of: 5¼" background square, 5¼" x 4¼" background rectangle, HST, HST, 5¼" x 4¼" background rectangle, 5¼" background square. Press seams open.

5. Attach strip units to the sides of the pieced center block (B). Press seams open.

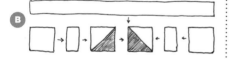

6. Attach 27" border strips to top and bottom of quilt. Press seams open. Attach 32" border strips to sides of quilt trimming excess if necessary. Press seams open.

ADD CORNERS

1. Draw a line diagonally from corner to corner on the WS of each 8" square corner piece.

2. Align a corner square on one quilt top corner RST (D). Sew on the drawn line. Trim seam allowance to ¼" using an acrylic ruler and a rotary cutter. Press triangle outward toward corner.

3. Repeat for the remaining three corners.

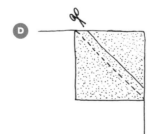

FINISHING

1. Layer backing, batting and quilt top together and baste.

2. Quilt as desired and attach binding using your favorite method. If quilt making is new to you, download the free PDF of Quilt Making Basics from the luckyspool.com website.

ROLL-UP PICNIC BLANKET

Of course you can take this on a picnic, but don't forget to take it with you on your next car trip, movie night in the park, or backyard adventure. The durable denim backing makes this a hardworking blanket adaptable to almost any outdoor event. Just a few simple steps and you've got a great family blanket to keep or gift!

style tips

▸ Make the bias tape scrappy! Cut 2" wide strips on the bias from scraps of varying lengths. Join the strips as you would for bias tape — you'll just have a lot more joining to do, but don't let that scare you off.

▸ A large-scale floral or even a vintage sheet would look amazing as the center panel.

MATERIALS

1¾ yards 54" wide fabric for center panel

2 yards 108" wide quilting cotton for background

1 yard quilting cotton for strap and binding

5 yards 44" wide lightweight denim for backing

6¼ yards 1" wide single fold bias tape OR additional 1 yard of quilting cotton if making your own (see page 62)

1 yard 20"-wide woven fusible interfacing (Pellon SF101)

2 yards 90" cotton or wool medium loft batting

(1) 1" button

length of thin string

buttonhole foot sewing machine attachment

water-soluble pen

10" plate or bowl for tracing curves

small plate or cup to trace strap curve

hand-sewing needle with large eye

perle cotton, size 8, for tying (optional)

CUTTING

From center fabric, cut:
    (1) 50" x 60" rectangle

From background fabric, cut:
    (1) 66" x 76" rectangle

From backing fabric, cut:
    (1) 5" x 31" strip for strap closure

From binding fabric, cut:
    (1) 5" x 31" strip for strap closure

    (8-10) 2 ½" bias cut strips for 290" of quilt bias binding

From interfacing, cut:
    5" x 31" strip for strap closure

SEAM ALLOWANCE

¼" unless otherwise noted

FINISHED SIZE

66" wide x 76" tall

instructions

PREPARE CENTER AND BACKGROUND

1. Fold center fabric in quarters and press. Repeat for background fabric.

2. Round each corner of center fabric using a 10" diameter plate or bowl. Align edge of plate to edges of corner and trace curved edge with a water-soluble pen. Cut along that line. (A)

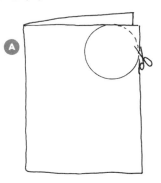

APPLY BIAS TAPE

1. Make 6¼ yards of 1" wide single fold bias tape if making your own.

2. Layer center fabric on top of background fabric using folds from Step 1 in *Prepare Center and Background* as a guide to help you align the two pieces where the fold creases match.

3. Pin 1" wide single fold bias tape in place, centering over the raw edge of center panel. Leaving a 6" tail unsewn, sew around center fabric perimeter close to each folded edge using a longer stitch length (2.8mm–3.0mm). Stop when 6" of raw edge remains. (B)

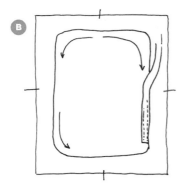

4. To join bias tape ends, overlap bias tape by 2", and trim any excess. (C)

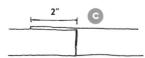

5. Unfold bias tape and rotate ends so they are RST and at a 90-degree angle to each other. Pin. Mark a line from one corner to the opposite. Sew on that line. Trim leaving a ¼" seam allowance. Press seam to side and finish attaching. (D)

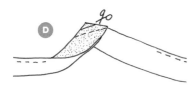

FINISH

1. Layer, backing, batting and top and hand-tie in a 3" grid using Pearle cotton thread (or quilt as desired).

2. To round out the corners of the quilt, first find the center of the smaller diameter circle from Step 2 of *Prepare Center and Background*. With a water-soluble pen on a string, hold the string at the center point and extend vertically from that point to meet the outer quilt edge. Using the pen and string as a compass, mark the section of the outer perimiter of the curve (E). Trim all four corners using this method.

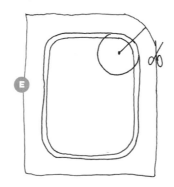

MAKE STRAP CLOSURE

1. Fuse interfacing to wrong side of binding strap closure.

2. Place strap rectangles RST. Mark curves on one end using a small cup and cut along drawn line through both strap pieces.

3. Keeping strap pieces RST, sew along sides and curved end (F), leaving short un-rounded end unsewn. Notch curves. Turn right side out. Press. Topstitch along sides and rounded end.

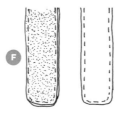

4. Center strap on back of quilt with aligning raw edges and with right sides facing up. Sew along short strap edge using a ⅛" seam allowance.

5. Fold the quilt into thirds. (G)

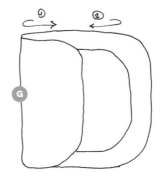

6. Roll and wrap strap around quilt. Make a mark where strap overlaps and sew buttonhole (see page 69) at mark. (H)

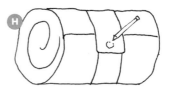

7. While still rolled up, mark through the buttonhole in the strap for the button placement. Attach button securely at mark. (I)

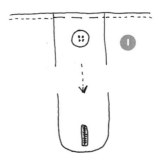

8. Attach the binding strips end to end pressing seams open. Fold in half, press, and attach using your favorite method, covering stitches and raw edge of strap. Your quilt is now ready for any outdoor event!

FLOOR POUF

Who doesn't love a floor pouf? They're everywhere you look! This one is great to use up small pieces of fabric, and the pieced top allows you to choose a variety of fabrics to coordinate with any space. I love how these poufs are low, but still cushy! Fill them with just about anything from polyfill to that bucket of fabric scraps in the corner of your closet — the handy zipper makes it easy to remove the fill and toss the cover in the wash. Make a few to stack in your living area and friends will always have a comfy place to rest.

style tips

▸ These work great for extra seating and lounging space. Making a set of two will balance out a room with not enough seats.

▸ Kids will love to use these for just about anything they can imagine. Have them help pick fabrics with you! You'll create something one-of-a-kind that they use and cherish.

MATERIALS

Strips: A variety of 2½" wide strips of quilting cotton for the top/bottom panels (totaling approximately 19 yards in length)

1¾ yards quilting cotton for the side panels (or ¾ yard 54" wide home dec fabric)

2½ yards 44" wide cotton canvas for stabilizer

1⅓ yards low-loft cotton batting (90" wide)

80 oz. or 5 lb. box of polyester filling (or filling of your choice, such as Cluster Stuff or even fabric scraps)

18" zipper

¼" fusible tape

water-soluble pen

pinking shears

zipper foot sewing machine attachment

walking foot sewing machine attachment (optional)

seam ripper

TIP: *Use up those extra quilt binding strips! The panels are the perfect size to use up odds and ends of leftover quilt binding. Or, dive into your scrap bin — this project is great for using up a ton of scrap strips.*

CUTTING

From strips, cut:
Approximately (115) 2½" strips in varying lengths from 6" to 12"

From side panel fabric, cut:
(4) 13½" x 24" rectangles for side panels

From canvas, cut:
(4) 13½" x 24" rectangles for side panels

(2) 24" squares for top/bottom panels

From batting, cut:
(4) 12½" x 23" rectangles for side panels

(2) 23" squares for top/bottom panels

SEAM ALLOWANCE
½" unless otherwise noted

FINISHED SIZE
23" wide x 23" deep x 13" tall

instructions

MAKE TOP AND BOTTOM PANELS

1. Sew strips together to join. To do this, place short strip ends perpendicular to each other and RST. Mark a line that runs diagonally from the upper left corner to lower right where the strips intersect. Pin. Sew along the marked line. Trim seam allowance to ¼" (A). Press seams open.

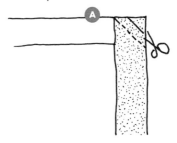

2. Repeat to make 12 pieced strips that are at least 24" long.

TIP: *Switch the angle of the sewn seams to create interest and movement on the panels.*

3. Using a ¼" seam allowance, sew together along long edges by placing RST until you have one 24" square panel, trimming to size if necessary (B). Press seams to one side.

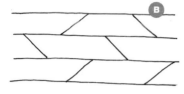

4. Repeat for Steps 1–3 for the second panel.

> **TIP**: *You wouldn't have to piece the bottom, but if you do, if one side gets a spill or stain, you can just flip the pouf over!*

5. Center the batting on top of the canvas. Layer top panel with top facing up. Spray or pin baste. Use the edge of your walking foot attachment or presser foot to quilt even parallel lines. I quilted lines ¾" apart, but feel free to experiment with different quilting designs. (C)

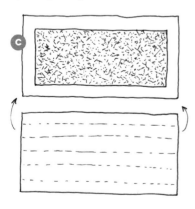

6. Repeat for bottom panel.

ASSEMBLE SIDE PANELS

1. Layer canvas, then center the batting. Layer the side panel right side up. Spray or pin baste. Quilt using your sewing machine's walking foot attachment, using the seams and the edge of the walking foot as a guide.

> **TIP**: *After spray basting, I used a Hera Marker to make diagonal lines from corner to opposite corner. I filled in each triangular section with quilting lines approximately ¼" apart. There are many other great quilting designs though, and since the side panels will move easily through your machine, this is a perfect opportunity to try something new!*

2. Repeat for remaining three side panels.

3. With a water-soluble pen on the WS of side panels mark a dot ½" away from each raw edge corner. With RST, join short sides of two side panels by sewing and stopping and backstitching at the dot. (D)

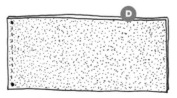

4. Repeat for the remaining two side panels.

5. Join all panels together. You will now have a large loop.

FINISH

1. Using a water-soluble pen, on the WS of top and bottom panels, mark dots ½" from all corners (E). Set top panel aside.

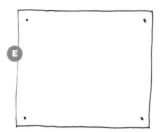

2. Join bottom to side panel loop. Align the bottom panel RST with one side panel, raw edges aligned. Begin sewing at a dot marked in Step 1 being sure to backstitch, then sew for 3". Switch to a longer basting stitch and baste until you reach 3" from the opposite marked dot. Switch back to a regular stitch length and sew up to the dot, being sure to backstitch. Press seam open. (F)

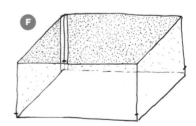

3. Center zipper right side down along pressed seam from Step 2 on top of basted seam allowance. Pin or fuse in place using ¼" fusible tape. Using your sewing machine's zipper foot, sew ¼" around all sides of zipper (G). Using a seam ripper on the right side of the fabric, gently remove basting stitches. You should now be able to open and close the zipper freely.

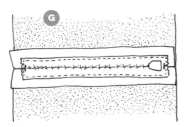

4. Sew opposite side of the bottom to its corresponding side panel, dot to dot while remembering to backstitch. Align sides to match the bottom panel and sew dot to dot again. The bottom will now be joined to all the side panels. Open zipper.

5. Join top to side panel loop. Align the top panel RST with one side panel, raw edges and dots aligned. Begin stitching at a dot marked in Step 1 being sure to backstitch. Sew along each side from dot to dot (aligning raw edges of top panel to corresponding side panels) around the entire pouf, being sure to backstitch again.

6. Finish all seams with a zigzag stitch if desired. Press all seams open.

7. Turn pouf right side out through the zipper opening and fill with polyfill or fabric scraps until the pouf is firm but not overstuffed. Now you'll really be sitting pretty!

PILLOW SET

These pillows will shine in any living space. A couple of quick pillows customized in your favorite colors and prints add instant style. Grab some fabrics from your stash and head to your living room to create the perfect palette. Inspired by art deco architecture with my own little twist, I designed these patterns to work well with any decor.

style tips

▸ Go crazy picking fabrics for these pillows! Muted colors and semi-solids will have an organic and soothing feel. Bright colors will energize your space.

▸ Make sure your fabrics don't blend together. High-contrasting fabrics work best for these designs.

MATERIALS
Long Pillow

(3) fat quarters quilting cotton (see assembly diagram page 124 for color placement)

½ yard quilting cotton for pillow back

1 yard muslin for pillow lining

½ yard low-loft cotton batting

20" invisible zipper

12" x 24" pillow form or stuffing

zipper foot sewing machine attachment OR

invisible zipper foot sewing machine attachment (optional)

Square Pillow

¾ yard for center and peg fabric

¾ yard for background fabric

⅛ yard for accent strips

(1) fat quarter quilting cotton for flying geese

¾ yard quilting cotton for backing

1½ yards muslin for pillow lining

¾ yard cotton batting

20" invisible zipper

24" square pillow form or stuffing

zipper foot sewing machine attachment OR

invisible zipper foot sewing machine attachment (optional)

SEAM ALLOWANCE
¼" unless otherwise noted

FINISHED SIZES
(1) 12"x 24" long pillow

(1) 24" square pillow

TIP: *Trouble finding a pillow form in the right size? Don't want to make a trip to the store? Try making your own form.*

1. *Cut two pieces 1" larger than your desired size from a fabric that won't show through your project, like muslin.*

2. *Sew RST with a ½" seam allowance leaving a 6" opening on one side.*

3. *Turn right side out through opening, stuff to desired fullness with polyester stuffing.*

4. *Sew opening closed by hand or by machine.*

instructions
FOR LONG PILLOW

CUTTING

All measurements are height x width.

From center panel fat quarter, cut:

(1) 12½" x 4½" rectangle

From accent fat quarter, cut:

(2) 12½" x 2" strips for accent strips

(3) 2" x 10" rectangles for pegs

From background fat quarter, cut:

(2) 12½" x 4½" rectangles

(2) 2" x 10" rectangles

(2) 2¾" x 10" rectangles

From muslin, cut:

(2) 12½" x 24½" rectangles for pillow linings

From batting and backing fabric, cut:

(1) 12½" x 24½" rectangle

STRIP-PIECE PEGS

1. Make pegs by alternating 10" x 2" peg and background rectangles — peg fabric, background, peg, background, peg — sewing together on long edges RST.

2. Sew 10" x 2¾" background rectangles to top and bottom of peg column you just made (A). Press seam allowances to darker fabric.

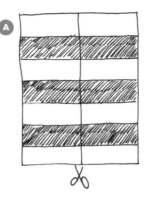

3. Cut completed peg column in half widthwise to form two 12½" x 5" columns.

SEW CENTER

1. Sew 12½" x 2" accent strips RST to center panel on the long edges (B). Press seam toward darker fabric.

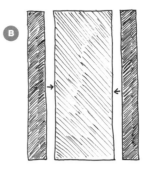

ASSEMBLE AND FINISH PILLOW TOP

1. Sew each peg column to its respective accent strip. Press seam toward accent strip.

2. Sew remaining background rectangles to either side of the peg columns (C). Press the seam open or toward the background fabric.

3. Quilt the pillow top panel by layering the muslin, batting and pillow top face up. I used straight lines to outline the accent fabrics. Serge or zig-zag all edges.

To finish, see *Putting Each Pillow Together* (page 127).

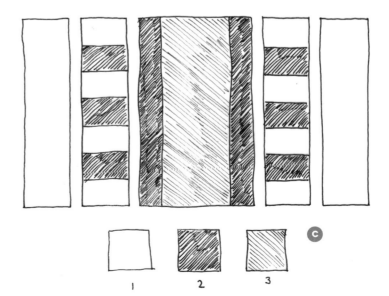

instructions

FOR SQUARE PILLOW

CUTTING

All measurements are height x width. Reference Figure K (see page 126).

From accent Fabric #3 (K), cut:
(2) 1½" x 24½" rectangles for accent strips

From center panel and peg Fabric #1 (K), cut:
(1) 4" x 12" rectangle for small pegs

(6) 7" x 3" rectangles for large pegs

(8) 2⅞" squares for flying geese background

(1) 4½" x 3" rectangle for flying geese column center

(2) 4½" x 3¼" rectangles for flying geese column ends

From flying geese Fabric #2 (K), cut:
(2) 5¼" squares for flying geese

From background Fabric #4 (K), cut:
(1) 3½" x 12" rectangle for small pegs

(12) 7" x 1¾" rectangles for large background pegs

(2) 24½" x 3" rectangles for outside border

(4) 7" x 3" rectangles for peg stack upper and lower

From muslin fabric, cut:
(2) 24½" squares for pillow linings

From batting and backing fabric, cut:
(1) 24½" square

STRIP-PIECE PEGS

1. Pair 3½" x 12" background and 4" x 12" center peg fabric RST. Sew along 12" length. Press seam to dark side.

2. Subcut 12" length into 8 equal pieces 1½" x 7" each. (D)

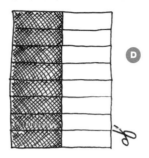

3. Create peg stack by sewing column (E). Use remaining pieces from Step 2 to create a second peg stack.

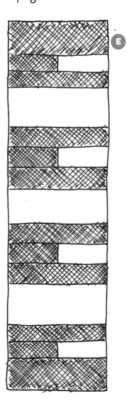

MAKE FLYING GEESE BLOCKS AND SEW CENTER COLUMN

1. Mark a diagonal line on the wrong side of (4) 2⅞" background fabric squares.

2. Pair two of the marked squares from Step 1 to opposite corners of the flying geese 5¼" square, slightly overlapping in the center. Pin and sew ¼" away from both sides of the marked diagonal lines. (F)

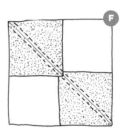

3. Cut the sewn unit on the marked line. You will have two units. Press the seam allowances and background fabric squares away from the background square and set one unit aside.

4. Add another 2⅞" square RST to one unit. Sew ¼" away from both sides of the marked diagonal line. Cut along the marked line (G). Repeat for the remaining unit from Step 3.

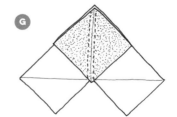

5. Press the seam allowances away from the flying geese fabric. You will now have four flying geese units. (H)

6. Repeat Steps 1–5 to make a total of 8 flying geese block units.

7. Assemble center panel column, using the flying geese units and their corresponding background fabrics. Add in the center rectangle and the two end rectangles to form a column. (I)

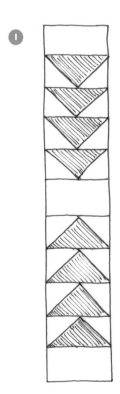

ASSEMBLE AND FINISH PILLOW TOP

1. Sew accent strips to both sides of center panel, RST. Press seams open. (J)

2. Sew peg stack to each side of accent strip. Press seams open.

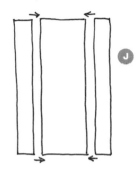

3. Sew a border piece to each long side of the peg stack. Press the seams to the dark side of the fabric. (K)

4. Quilt the pillow top panel by layering the muslin, batting and pillow top face up. I used straight lines to outline the flying geese and the pegs.

5. Serge or zig-zag stitch along all edges.

PUTTING EACH PILLOW TOGETHER

ATTACH PILLOW BACK

1. Place pillow back WST with muslin.

2. Serge or use a zig-zag stitch along all edges to secure the layers.

INSERT INVISIBLE ZIPPER

1. Place assembled pillow top right side up with top of pillow farthest away from you. Press invisible zip with iron. Open invisible zipper.

2. Place zipper right side down on the pillow's bottom edge, aligning edge of zipper tape to raw edge of pillow. Pin in place.

3. Using either a zipper foot attachment or an invisible zipper foot attachment, sew as close to zipper teeth as you feel comfortable. Backstitch at both start and stop ends. Close zipper. (L)

TIP: *When installing an invisible zipper, although a regular zipper foot will certainly work, an invisible zipper foot is specifically designed for the task. This specialty foot will take a lot of the guess work out of installation. It has 'channels' that the zipper teeth follow and thus guide the stitching perfectly. I find that the invisible zipper foot is well worth the investment.*

4. With the pillow back right side up, center long zipper tape edges along bottom raw edge, with zipper right side down. Pillow fabrics will be RST. Pin zipper in place (M). Sew, remembering to backstitch.

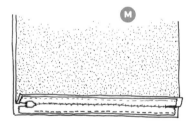

5. Close zipper halfway. Align pillow top and back so all raw edges are aligned, RST. At the beginning and end of zipper, pull zipper tape up and out of the way of the seam allowance. Pin from zipper end around pillow edges to zipper start. Sew, using a ½" seam allowance and backstitching at both ends on either side of the zipper. (N)

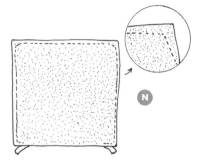

TIP: *It helps to taper to a slightly larger seam allowance at each corner to give the pillow a nice snug fit.*

TRIM AND FILL

1. Trim corners with pinking shears to approximately ¼" seam allowance.

2. Turn pillow right side out, making sure the corners are turned nicely. Press and insert pillow form and place in your favorite comfy spot.

BASKET

Dress up your shelves in style with this fun-to-construct basket. In no time, you can have a shelf of baskets lined up, made of the fabrics you love, plus have the extra hidden storage space that always comes in handy. Toys, fabric scraps, toiletries, craft supplies, or yarn would all feel right at home in these baskets. Sturdy leather handles are a breeze to sew and give the basket a professional finished look that'll fit any decor.

style tips

▸ Think bold and beautiful when making your fabric selections. These baskets are big enough that a large-scale print really gets a chance to shine! Consider adding piping to the front and back panels too.

▸ If you can't find leather straps when you need them: make fabric ones instead!

MATERIALS

½ yard 54" wide medium-weight cotton (twill, denim, canvas, home dec) or ¾ yard 44" wide fabric for exterior

¾ yard quilting cotton for lining

12" square quilting cotton for handle cover

1½ yard heavyweight double-sided fusible stabilizer (Pellon 72F)

Fusible woven interfacing scraps, at least (2) 3" x 6" pieces

16" long x ½" wide leather strap, cut into two equal lenghts

tracing paper

water-soluble pen

turning tool

pinking shears

CUTTING

See pullout for pattern pieces. Trace and cut the required pieces.

All measurements are height x width.

From exterior fabric, cut:
(2) Front/Back patterns

(1) 12" x 27⅝" rectangle for exterior wall

From 12" square of quilting cotton, cut:

(4) 2½" x 5¾" rectangles for handle covers

From lining fabric, cut:
(2) Front/Back patterns cut to indicated line

(1) 11" x 26⅝" rectangle for interior wall

From stabilizer, cut:
(2) Front/Back patterns (trim to stitch line as marked on pattern piece)

(1) 11" x 26⅝" rectangle for wall

From interfacing, cut:
(2) 2½" x 5¾" rectangles for handle covers

SEAM ALLOWANCE
½" unless otherwise noted

FINISHED SIZE
9" tall x 10" wide x 11" deep

instructions

Transfer all markings from pattern pieces.

MAKE EXTERIOR AND LINING

1. Finger press in half to find center of long side of exterior wall and bottom center of the front/back panels. Mark with a water-soluble pen within the seam allowance.

2. Align center markings of wall and front panel and pin in place, RST. Match top corners of wall and front panel and pin in place. Pin along entire raw edge. As you get to the curves, clip into the seam allowance (about ¼"–⅜") of the wall piece to ease around corner of front panel. Pin and sew. (A)

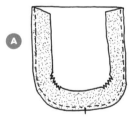

3. Repeat Steps 1–2 to attach back panel to the wall.

4. Press seams toward wall panel.

5. Repeat Steps 1–4 using lining pieces.

6. Trim curved seam allowances to ¼". Pinking shears are a great tool to use for this step. Press side seams open.

ASSEMBLE

1. Place lining into exterior RST. Pin and sew around top opening. Leave a 10" opening on one side and backstitch at both ends (B). Turn right side out through opening.

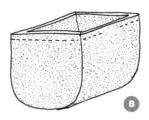

2. Press well along top edge. Insert and position back panel fusible stabilizer through opening. Fuse into place from both sides of back panel. (C)

TIP: *Use a few long pins to help hold everything in place as you fuse.*

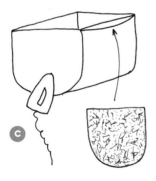

3. Repeat for front panel fusible stabilizer and front panel. Set aside.

MAKE HANDLE COVERS AND ATTACH

1. Fuse interfacing to the wrong side of one exterior handle cover piece. Place RST with the non-interfaced handle cover piece. Sew along all edges, leaving a 2"–3" opening along one long side for turning. Clip corners. Turn right side out. Gently push out corners (I like to use a chopstick). Press, enclosing the raw edges of the opening.

2. Pin into place on the back exterior panel with top edge of handle cover ¾" down from top finished edge and centered approximately 2⅝" from each edge. Insert ends of leather strap down into handle cover about ½" from both handle cover sides and pin in place. Topstitch around entire handle cover going slowly over where the leather strap is inserted. (D)

3. Repeat Steps 1–2 with remaining handle cover and leather strap on front exterior panel.

FINISH

1. Insert wall fusible stabilizer into opening. Smooth and adjust with your hands. Fuse in place from both sides. (E)

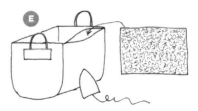

TIP: *Don't look for perfection here. It can be a bit tricky. Focus on getting the exterior as smooth and wrinkle-free as you can.*

2. Hand stitch the opening closed using a hidden stitch (the fusible stabilizer will hold everything in place) or topstitch along the entire opening of the basket using a long stitch length and moving the handles out of the way as you sew.

3. Press again to reshape the basket and fill with all those things that you could never find a home for.

CARRY-ALL PINCUSHION

Never lose that tailor's chalk or misplace your measuring tape again. This fast and friendly pincushion packs a punch! It holds all of your must-have favorites so that they're within easy reach and organized. It is also great to bring along to workshops and classes. This project is quick and makes a great gift for anyone who sews. Don't we all love a good pincushion?

style tips

▸ This is a great project to construct using your most precious scraps — just press well and use spray starch to get your pieces ready to go.
▸ Try making all the pockets in a single fabric instead of a mix, to transform the pincushion into a more sleek and modern style.

MATERIALS

(1) fat eighth quilting cotton for main body sides/end

(1) fat eighth quilting cotton for top/bottom

(1) fat quarter quilting cotton for pockets/scissors strap (or use scraps)

¼ yard ByAnnie's Soft and Stable interfacing (or fusible fleece can also be a good substitute in this project)

¼ yard woven fusible interfacing (such as Pellon SF101 - 20"-wide)

5 oz. polyfill stuffing

crushed walnut shells

water-soluble pen

tracing paper

TIP: *Crushed walnut shells might seem a little odd. You can readily find them in the pet bedding section of a pet store. The walnut shells add weight to stabilize the pincushion, and they also sharpen the pin tip with each poke!*

CUTTING

See pullout for pattern pieces. Trace and cut the required pieces.

All measurements are height x width.

From main body sides/end fabric, cut:
  (2) 4" x 4½" rectangles for end panels
  (2) 4" x 9" rectangles for side panels

From top and bottom fabric, cut:
  (2) 4½" x 9" rectangles for top/bottom panels

From pocket fabric, cut:
  (4) 3½" x 4½" rectangles for end pockets
  (2) 4" x 6" rectangles for slip pocket
  (2) 3½" x 13" rectangles for pleated pocket
  (1) 2" x 4½" rectangle for scissors strap

TIP: *You may also choose to dive into your scrap pile for these pocket fabric requirements. Many of the pieces are small, so this project is perfect for using your favorite scraps.*

From ByAnnie's Soft and Stable, cut:
  (2) 9" x 4" rectangles for side panels

From interfacing, cut:
  (2) 4" x 4½" rectangles for end panels
  (2) 9" x 4½" rectangles for top/bottom panels

SEAM ALLOWANCE
½" unless otherwise noted

FINISHED SIZE
3" tall x 8" wide x 3½" deep

instructions

Transfer all markings from pattern pieces.

PREPARE SIDE AND TOP/BOTTOM PANELS

1. Baste ByAnnie's Soft and Stable interfacing to wrong side of both side panels using a ¼" seam allowance.

2. Fuse interfacing to end panels and top/bottom panels. Set aside.

MAKE POCKETS

1. Place slip pocket panels RST. Sew along one short end. Position fabrics WST and press. Topstitch along that seam. (A)

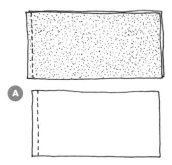

2. Align assembled slip pocket to right side of one side panel aligning raw edges on one short side. Baste in place on top, bottom and side of pocket.

3. Using a water-soluble pen, mark a line down the horizontal center of the slip pocket. Sew along the drawn line, dividing the slip pocket in two being sure to backstitch at the top edge of slip pocket to reinforce the seam (B). Set aside.

4. Place two end pocket panels RST. Mark curved line using pattern piece. Sew along marked line. Trim seam allowance to ¼". Clip curve. Position fabrics WST and press. Topstitch along the curved seam. (C)

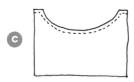

5. Align assembled end pocket to right side of one end panel, aligning along the bottom. Baste in place on sides and bottom, using ¼" seam allowance. Set aside.

6. Repeat for the second end pocket/end panel unit. (D)

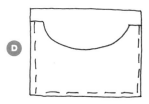

7. Place two pleated pocket panels RST. Sew along top long edge. Position fabrics WST and press. Topstitch along top of the pocket.

8. Mark vertical center of pleated pocket. From center make another mark 1" away on one side. Bring 1" marking to center and press. Repeat for other side. Edge stitch along each pleat fold to hold it in place. Along bottom edge, mark 1½" and ½" from each short end. (E)

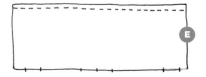

9. Fold so the markings meet, pressing pleat toward short end. Edge stitch along pleat fold. Repeat on the opposite side (F). Pin pleats into place.

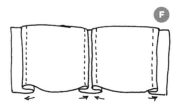

10. Baste all pleats into place along bottom raw edge, using ¼" seam allowance.

11. Align pleated pocket to remaining side panel along bottom and sides. Baste in place using a ¼" seam allowance. Sew on vertical center line marked in Step 8 through all layers, dividing pocket in two being sure to backstitch at the top edge of the pleated pocket to reinforce the seam (G). Set aside.

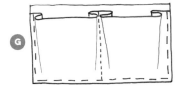

MAKE SCISSORS STRAP

1. Press strap in half lengthwise, WST. Open up and press raw edges WST to center line. Fold in half again and press. Topstitch along both long sides of the strap.

2. Mark a line 3½" from one short edge of top panel. Align inner edge of strap to that line and baste strap short edges to top panel using a ¼" seam allowance.

ASSEMBLE

1. On WS of each assembled side and end panel, mark a dot ½" from each corner. (H)

2. Join short ends of the 4 assembled side and end panels to form a loop, alternating side and end panels. Sew RST from one marked dot to the other, being sure to backstitch as you sew. Ensure that the pleated and end pocket openings are facing the same direction. (I)

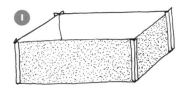

3. Aligning the long raw edges, join top to side panel. Sew from dot to dot. Repeat for remaining side and end panels, sewing from dot to dot. (J)

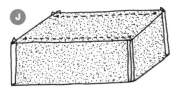

TIP: *Make sure pocket openings are facing top panel.*

4. Join bottom to side and end panels as in Step 3, but leaving a 3" opening on one side panel (K) and backstitching at both sides of the opening.

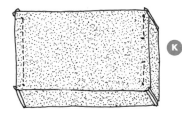

5. Clip corners. Turn right side out through opening. Push out corners (I like to use a chopstick). Stuff to your desired fullness with a combination of crushed walnut shells and polyfill, then hand stitch opening closed using a whipstitch or similar. Looks sharp, right?

TIP: *If you'd like, make a small pouch from scrap fabric to contain the crushed walnut shells. Cut two rectangles the same size as the top/bottom panels. Place the rectangles RST and sew along edges with a ½" seam allowance, leaving a 4" opening on one side. Turn right side out and fill with crushed walnut shells. Sew opening closed by hand or by machine. When you have the pincushion assembled, put the walnut shell pouch into the pincushion near the top and fill the rest of the space with polyfill.*

<> QUILT

Designing this quilt was the ultimate fun time. I wanted a quilt that would work well in my own mid-century modern bedroom. I wanted it to have a bold central design, making this quilt the only decorative element you would need in a room. The blocks are made using freezer paper piecing, which will add another great technique to your piecing repertoire. Because this pattern features large shapes, it is a great skill-builder and will open up a world full of possibilities with freezer paper piecing.

style tips

▸ Choosing fabrics for this quilt will give you the control you need to fit your style perfectly. Mix up the background fabric colors and invite a whole new design.

▸ Striped fabric can be a design element in itself — consider piecing each of the blocks using a different colored striped fabric.

MATERIALS

Fabric A: 3 yards quilting cotton

Fabric B: 6¾ yards quilting cotton for background

¾ yard quilting cotton for binding

5½ yards quilting cotton for backing

2¾ yards of 90" wide cotton batting

freezer paper

pencil

36" ruler (optional)

TIP: *You can use all one fabric from Fabric A or divide it up. Reference cutting layout (see page 141) to help visualize how you can make changes. My version used 2 yards of one light value print and one yard of another light value print.*

NOTE: *Freezer paper may be better known for wrapping up food to protect it from freezer burn, but it has many other great uses! The freezer paper piecing process is simple. First you trace or draw the pieces of your pattern with a pencil on the matte side of the freezer paper, then cut them out. Next, iron the pattern to the wrong side of your fabric. Cut around the paper, leaving a ¼" seam allowance all the way around. The freezer paper can be pulled from the fabric once the block is completed and ironed again for the next block.*

CUTTING

See *Make Pattern Pieces* for triangle cutting instructions (page 134).

From Fabric A, cut:
(6) Pattern 2 and (6) Pattern 2B triangles

From Fabric B, cut:
3 yards for cutting all Pattern 1 and 3 triangles, subcut into:
(6) Pattern 1 triangles
(6) Pattern 1B triangles
(6) Pattern 3 triangles
(6) Pattern 3B triangles

(6) 2½" x WOF strips, subcut to (6) 2½" x 30½" strips for A sashing

(4) 3½" x WOF strips, subcut to (4) 3½" x 30½" strips for B sashing

(2) 2½" x WOF strips, subcut to (2) 2½" x 33½" strips for C sashing

(4) 8½" x WOF strips, subcut to (4) 8½" x 33½" strips for side borders

(4) 12½" x WOF strips, subcut to (4) 12½" x 31" strips for top and bottom borders

From binding fabric, cut:
(9) 2½" x WOF strips

SEAM ALLOWANCE
¼" unless otherwise noted

FINISHED SIZE
78" x 90"

instructions

MAKE PATTERN PIECES

1. Using a ruler, draw a 30" wide x 9" tall rectangle on the matte side of a length of freezer paper. Referring to Figure A, make a diagonal line from the upper left corner to the lower right. Measure in 12½" from the bottom left of your paper and make a mark. Draw a diagonal line from the upper left corner to the mark. Referencing Figure A, transfer tick marks as indicated and number each of the three Pattern pieces 1-3.

2. Repeat using the mirror image of Figure A and labeling the segments 1B, 2B, and 3B.

3. Cut out the six freezer paper patterns along the drawn lines.

4. Iron Pattern 2 and 2B onto Fabric A and cut out ¼" around each shape (B).

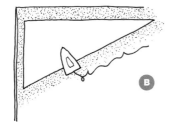

5. Remove freezer paper and reuse, repeating to create a total of (6) of each pattern piece OR leave the freezer paper adhered to stabilize the fabric while sewing. If doing the latter, you will be assembling the blocks one at a time. The illustrations that follow use the single block construction method with the paper intact to help add clarity to the piecing process.

6. Iron Pattern 1, 1B, 3, and 3B onto Fabric B and cut out ¼" around each shape. Remove freezer paper from fabric and reuse, repeating to create a total of (6) of each pattern piece.

7. If piecing the blocks in groups (as opposed to the single block construction in Step 5), separate triangles into six groups by their numbers transferred from Step 1.

> **TIP:** *It may take you longer to prep these pieces than to actually assemble the blocks together. Remember to handle the pieces carefully as there will be bias edges that may distort with handling. Take your time and don't be hard on yourself. If you are a fan of spray starch, now is the time to use it to give those blocks more stability when piecing. Large blocks like these take a little more handling time and patience. I definitely recommend making a test block or two with practice fabric to get a feel for the process.*

PIECE BLOCKS

1. Pin all block pieces RST. Align by pinning through tick marks transferred from Step 4, and sew using a small stitch length (2.0mm). Begin piecing each block by sewing Fabric B triangle 1 to Fabric A triangle 2 (C), then Fabric B triangle 3 to Fabric A triangle 2 (D). Repeat to create 6 Block A units.

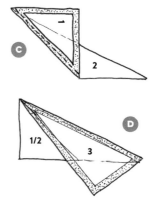

2. Repeat with the mirror image triangle units to create 6 Block B units.

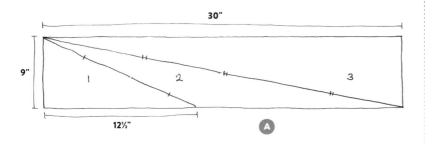

3. Press seams open.

4. Trim seam allowances at points to ⅛" to reduce bulk, being careful not to clip through any stitching.

5. You will now have a total of 12 blocks measuring 9½" x 30½" unfinished: 6 Block A units using the pattern orientation and 6 Block B units using its mirror image. (E)

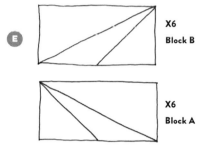

X6
Block B

X6
Block A

ASSEMBLE

Attach sashings A and B to form two columns. Join the two columns by attaching sashing C. Attach each of the borders as indicated in Quilt Assembly Diagram at right.

> **NOTE:** *You will need to join the strips as necessary and trim any excess fabric. Press all seams open as you work.*

FINISHING

1. Layer backing, batting and quilt top together and baste.

2. Quilt as desired and attach binding using your favorite method. If quilt making is new to you, download the free PDF of Quilt Making Basics from the luckyspool.com website.

QUILT ASSEMBLY DIAGRAM

PATCHWORK BENCH

Why not make a fun bench that perfectly suits the style of your home? This is a great intro-to-woodworking project that uses just a few small hand tools and materials from your local home improvement store and craft store. Plus it's a fun way to use up some scraps and end up with a beautiful finished project featuring your favorite patchwork.

style tips

▸ Take your time shopping for legs for this piece. Parsons legs are square and have clean lines. I used tapered legs, but the choice is up to you and what fits with your style.

▸ Stain or paint the legs for different looks.

▸ Instead of a square grid patchwork for the top, mix it up! Leftover quilt blocks would be beautiful pieced together.

MATERIALS
Frame

16" x 36" piece of ¾" plywood

(4) 8" table/bench legs

(4) leg mounting plates (straight top plate)

2" x 18" x 10' regular density urethane foam

1 yard 90" wide Polyester batting

staple gun and staples

spray adhesive

100 grit sandpaper

palm sander (optional)

electric knife

water-soluble pen

Fabric cover

1¼ yard 54" wide medium-weight cotton (home dec weight, etc.) for sides

(36) 4½" squares from a variety of quilting cottons for patchwork top

4 yards fusible woven interfacing (20"-wide)

CUTTING
From medium-weight cotton, cut:

(2) 12" x 36½" rectangles for long sides

(2) 12" x 16½" rectangles for short sides

From interfacing, cut:

(1) 36½" x 16½" rectangle for top

(2) 12" x 36½" rectangles for long sides

(2) 12" x 16½" rectangles for short sides

SEAM ALLOWANCE
¼" unless otherwise noted

FINISHED SIZE
15½" tall (including legs) x 36" wide x 16" deep

instructions

MAKE COVER

1. Piece 4½" squares to create patchwork top consisting of 9 columns and 4 rows. Press seams open. Finished top should measure 16½" x 36½". Press entire piece.

2. Fuse interfacing to wrong side of top and each side piece.

3. On WS of each side piece, with a water-soluble pen mark a dot ⅜" from each corner. Place one short side piece and one long side piece RST and with a ⅜" seam allowance sew along short side beginning at the marked dot, remembering to backstitch (A). Repeat for remaining short and long side pieces.

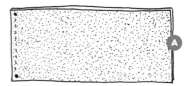

4. Beginning at the marked dot, join assembled long side to assembled short side RST, sewing along short side, remembering to backstitch. Repeat for remaining long and short sides to form a loop.

5. With a ⅜" seam allowance, sew assembled sides to top. Align top to sides RST and sew along both long edges. Sew from marked dot to marked dot on each side. Repeat by aligning short sides to corresponding top short sides and sewing from dot to dot. Reinforce seams with zig-zag stitch or serger.

6. Press bottom edge of cover up 1" to the wrong side. Sew in place (B). The cover is now complete.

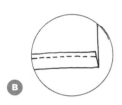

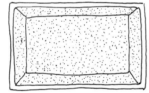

BUILD BENCH BASE

1. Using 100 grit sandpaper, sand all plywood corners as well as top and bottom surfaces. (You can either do this with a palm sander or the old-fashioned way by hand.)

2. Following manufacturer instructions, install a leg mounting plate 1" from each corner. Typical installation includes four screws and a metal plate. (C)

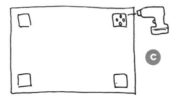

3. Using an electric knife, cut foam into (3) 16" x 36" pieces.

4. Outside or in a well-ventilated area, use spray adhesive to attach first layer of foam to plywood. Continue using adhesive to attach remaining two layers of foam on top of first layer until you have three layers adhered.

5. Wrap assembled foam and plywood using a double layer of polyester batting, being careful to avoid any wrinkles in the batting. With a staple gun, attach batting to underside of plywood. (D)

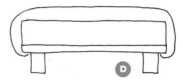

ASSEMBLE

1. Slip fabric cover over assembled base.

2. Wrap corners, tucking in short sides first then long sides. Use staple gun to attach cover to underside of plywood, stapling within the hem of the cover where possible.

3. Attach legs. You may need to cut a small hole in the cover sides for the leg to easily attach to the mounting plate. Use sharp scissors and awl to mark placement. Screw in legs, place under a sunny window and put up your feet.

glossary

CLIPPED CORNERS
Use scissors and clip across a corner when the stitching is a 90 degree angle. Reduces bulk at the corner when project is turned right side out.

BOXED CORNERS
Refers to the 'gusset' of a bag. Usually controls how deep the bag will be.

NOTCHED CURVES
Using sharp scissors, cutting 'v' shapes into the seam allowance on a convex curve. For concave curves simply use scissors to snip into the seam allowance. It is important not to cut the stitching in either instance. See also: Pinking Shears

DOUBLE FOLD BIAS TAPE
Great for concealing raw edges. Double fold is when bias strips are joined to create a determined length. The raw edges are folded to the center, then the whole tape is pressed in half again.

SINGLE FOLD BIAS TAPE
Single fold bias tape is great for flat work and is used on the Roll-Up Picnic Blanket project. Bias strips are joined to create a specified length, the raw edges are folded to meet at the center.

HOME DÉCOR FABRIC (HOME DEC)
Home dec fabric is a heavier weight than quilting cotton. It's ideal for home decor projects such as pillows and upholstery. Also a durable and sturdy fabric choice for a bag or tote.

FAT QUARTER (FQ)
An 18" x 22" piece of fabric cut by quilt shops. A great way to have a diverse stash without having full ½ yard cuts.

RIGHT SIDES TOGETHER (RST)
Right sides together refers to placing the right side of a fabric facing the right side of another piece of fabric.

WRONG SIDES TOGETHER (WST)
Same as RST, but matching wrong sides of the fabric.

TOPSTITCH
Visible stitching on the outside of a project, topstitching is usually ⅛" away from the edge of a seam. It reinforces the seam. I recommend a stitch length of 3.0mm.

EDGE STITCH
Similar to a topstitch, but usually on the edge of a seam and approx. ¹⁄₁₆" away from folded edge. Many machines have an edge stitching foot that utilizes a special guide bar.

TEETH SIDE DOWN
This refers to the top of a zipper. If you hold a zipper and are able to use the zipper pull to open it, then you're looking at the right side (or top/teeth side) of the zipper. If you can't open the zipper, then it's teeth side down.

BASTE
This covers two sewing techniques. Baste can refer to a longer stitch length (usually 5.0mm) sewn within the seam allowance to temporarily hold two or more pieces of fabric together. Or, in quilt making, it refers to how a quilt sandwich is held together, usually by curved safety pins, spray baste, or thread.

HALF SQUARE TRIANGLES (HST)
Popular for construction of many quilt blocks. At its simplest, a half-square triangle is a square divided in half diagonally, and usually features two different fabrics.

PINKING SHEARS
Specialty scissors that cut a zig-zag instead of a straight cut. Great for finishing seams inside a garment quickly, keeps seams from fraying during wash cycles. For curves, instead of clipping notches, pinking shears can be a great stand-in for getting the job done quickly.

SERGER

A 4 thread sewing machine for finishing raw edges of fabric to prevent fraying. Most trim the seam allowance while sewing the seam. I recommend an entry level serger to anyone who likes making pillows or garments.

ZIPPER FOOT

Specialty sewing machine foot that allows the needle to get close to the edge of a zipper.

WALKING FOOT

Specialty sewing machine foot that has extra mechanical feet on the top. Allows fabric to be pulled evenly through the machine. Great for straight line quilting and also any kind of project that uses topstitching or has thick layers.

WATER-SOLUBLE PEN

My most preferred tool for temporarily marking fabric. The marking disappears with water. Follow manufacturers instructions carefully.

WOVEN FUSIBLE INTERFACING

Woven interfacing is an interfacing that is 100% cotton. My favorite is Pellon Shape-Flex SF101.

FUSIBLE INTERFACING

Interfacing with a special glue that adheres the interfacing to fabric with the heat of an iron.

FUSIBLE FLEECE

Interfacing that is fusible and is approximately ¼" thick. Great for adding a little structure or body to a project.

SHOT COTTON

Cotton fabric that is woven using one color for the weft threads and a coordinating/contrasting thread for the warp threads. Great for garments. It has a beautiful drape and a soft hand. The different threads make a subtle almost shimmery effect. Great for quilting too!

FREE MOTION QUILTING

Using a darning foot on a home sewing machine, a quilt is quilted in an infinite number of design choices. Allows the user to create designs by essentially 'drawing' a design with thread.

STRAIGHT LINE QUILTING

Quilting with straight lines, usually a walking foot is preferred. Spacing between quilting lines and designs vary.

BAR TACK

Essentially a tight zig-zag stitch that is used to 'tack' layers of fabric in place.

TICK MARKS

Marks to help align quilting blocks.

QUILT-AS-YOU-GO

Method of machine quilting that works in small segments. Layering fabric and quilting small portions at a time.

SPRAY STARCH

One of my essential tools for sewing. Spray starch is sprayed on the fabric and then ironed to give it more body and become crisper. Also releases wrinkles.

STAY STITCH

Sewn within the seam allowance on a curved edge before construction to prevent unwanted stretching.

ON THE BIAS

On the bias means to cut the fabric on a 45 degree angle to the selvedge. This allows fabric to go around curves without puckering.

COTTON CORDING

You can find packaged cotton cording in the notions section of your favorite fabric store, or my favorite place — the home improvement store. Cording is used when making piping.

FUSIBLE TAPE

Also called Hem Tape. This is a great product to have on hand. It's a double-sided adhesive strip that comes on rolls in a variety of widths. My favorite width is ¼". Not only does it help make perfect piping, but also you'll find it's great for installing zippers, for holding bias tape in place and hemming! Go grab some now if you don't have it already.

WOF

Width of Fabric (assumes 42"–45" wide).

resources

Robert Kaufman Fabrics

Pellon

Pink Castle Fabrics

Pacific Trimmings – cord stops, zippers, bag hardware

Buckleguy.com – bag hardware, grommets, rivets, zippers

Snapsource.com – metal snaps and setting tool

Hawthorne Threads

Maze & Vale

Umbrella Prints

Vandermeer & Jones

Fancy Tiger Crafts

Nido

Fabricworm

Wawak – zippers, general sewing supplies

ETSY RESOURCES:

Skinnylaminx

MissMatatabi

FreshModernFabric

Zipit – zippers

Sewingsupplies – magnetic snaps, bag hardware, twill tape

BeingBags – magnetic snaps, bag hardware

AllLeatherSupplies – leather straps

MinkusMargo – grommets, rivets, press

Goldenagebeads – jewelry findings

KallyCo – jewelry findings

STANDARD BODY MEASUREMENTS												
	XSmall		Small		Medium		Large		XLarge		2XLarge	
Size	2	4	6	8	10	12	14	16	18	20	22	24
Bust	32	33	34	35	36	37	39	40½	42½	44½	50	52
Waist	24	25	26	27	28	29	31	32½	34½	36½	42½	44½
Hips	34	35½	36½	37½	38½	40	41½	43	45	47	52½	54½

<> QUILT

light colored fabric — 3 yards total

background fabric —
12 of each shape (2 yards total)

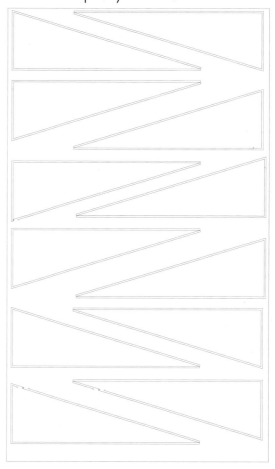

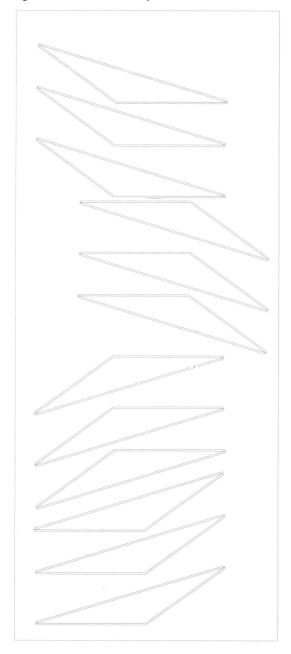

background fabric — 12 of
each shape (1 yard total)

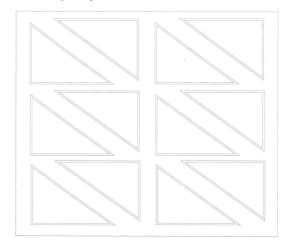

CHAMBRAY DRESS

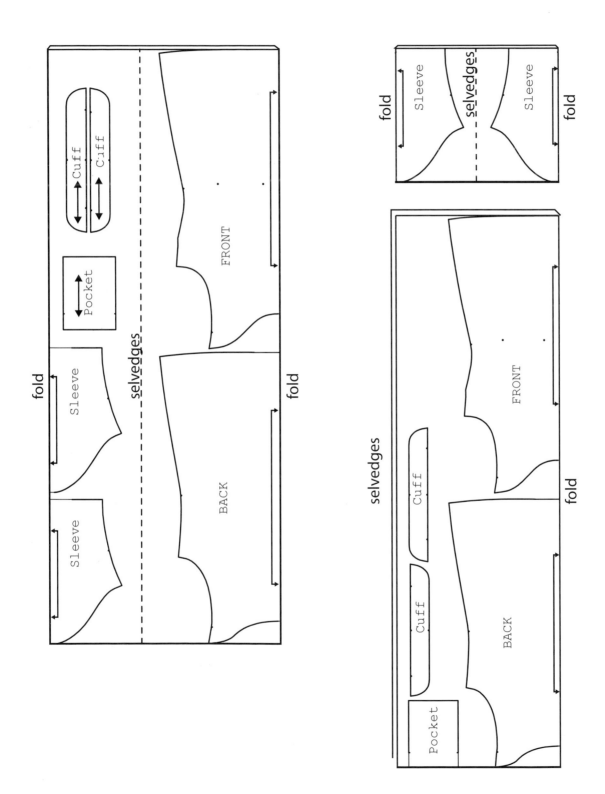

WOMEN'S TUNIC

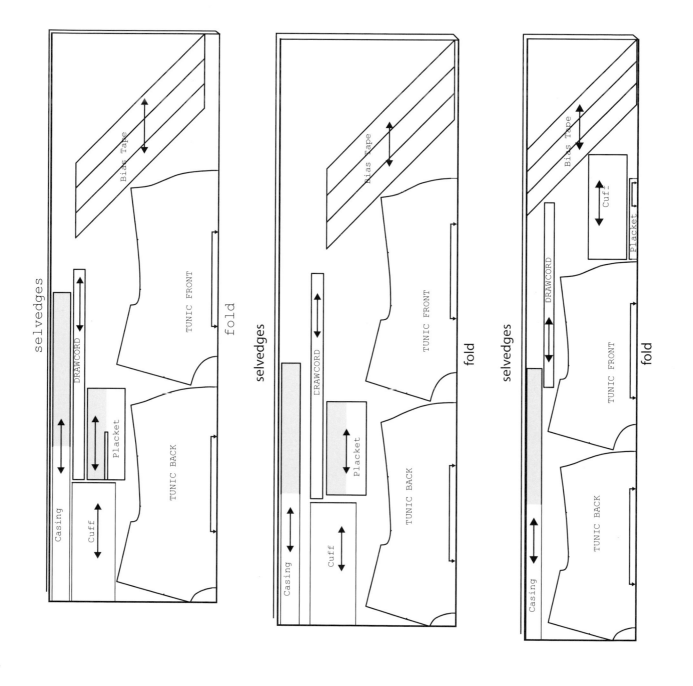

acknowledgments

Thank you to my husband for always listening and being my voice of reason when I couldn't find my own.

Thank you to my mom and dad for your support and understanding, for always being there for me. And thanks mom for showing me the ropes when it came to learning how to sew.

Thank you to my friend Holly DeGroot, I so appreciated your expert eye and photography skills and of course your friendship. And thanks for letting me drag you all around town, make you stand on chairs, and withstand Wisconsin humidity for that perfect shot.

Thank you to my friend Raina who was such a great sport to model for me. And to my friend Jill and her son Zeke who added that extra touch of innocent cuteness to my quilt picture.

Thank you to Pellon for providing interfacing for all of the projects in this book and to Robert Kaufman Fabrics for providing many of the fabrics used throughout. Thank you for your enthusiasm and support.

Thank you to my friend Christina Lane who gorgeously quilted the < > Quilt and the Up & Down Quilt. Thank you, Christina, for adding your creative touch to those.

Thank you to my fantastic pattern testers who provided invaluable feedback on a tight timeline. Thank you to everyone who's eyes and hands touched this project, I couldn't have done it without you.

Thank you to everyone who has ever stopped by my blog to leave kind and encouraging comments and support. This book is for you.

Anna